# Emotional Intelligence

*2 Books in 1: The Ultimate Guide to Improve Your Mind. Discover Effective Problem-Solving and Critical Thinking Strategies to Finally Master Your Emotions and Social Skills.*

**Edward Anderson, Jennet Brown**

**ISBN: 978-1-80271-095-3**

processes, or Instructions contained within is the solitary and utter responsibility of the recipient reader. Under no circumstances will any legal responsibility or blame be held against the publisher for any reparation, damages, or monetary loss due to the information herein, either directly or indirectly.

Respective authors own all copyrights not held by the publisher.

The information herein is offered for informational purposes solely and is universal as such. The presentation of the information is without a contract or any type of guarantee assurance.

The trademarks that are used are without any consent, and the publication of the trademark is without permission or backing by the trademark owner. All trademarks and brands within this book are for clarifying purposes only and are owned by the owners themselves, not affiliated with this document.

# Table of Contents

# PART 1

# Emotional Intelligence

*The Ultimate Guide to Build Healthy Relationships. Learn How to Master your Emotions to Finally improve Your EQ and Social Skills.*

**Edward Anderson**

## Introduction

Emotional intelligence (EI), and emotional intelligence quotient (EQ) is the capacity of people to perceive their own emotions, and those of others, recognize between different sentiments, and name them suitably, utilize emotional data to control thinking, and conduct, and change feelings to adjust to conditions. The term initially showed up in 1964; it acquired fame in the 1995 top-rated book Emotional Intelligence, composed by science writer Goleman. Goleman characterized EI as the variety of abilities, and qualities that drive administration execution.

Different models have been created to quantify EI. The attribute model, developed by Konstantinos V. Petrides in 2001, centers around self-announcing of conduct airs, and saw capacities. The capacity model, created by Peter Salovey and John Mayer in 2004, centers around the person's ability to deal with emotional data and explore the social climate. Goleman's unique model may now be viewed as a blended model that joins what has been demonstrated independently as capacity EI, and quality EI. Later exploration has zeroed in on feeling acknowledgment, which alludes to emotional states' attribution dependent on perceptions of visual and hear-able nonverbal signs. Also, neurological examinations have tried to portray the neural instruments of emotional intelligence.

Studies have shown that individuals with high EI have more noteworthy psychological wellness, work execution and administration abilities, albeit no causal connections have appeared. EI is regularly connected with compassion since it includes individual interfacing their encounters with those of others. Since its advocacy in late many years, creating EI strategies has gotten broadly looked for by people trying to turn out to be more viable pioneers.

Reactions have fixated on whether EI is natural intelligence, and whether it has gradual legitimacy over IQ, and the Big Five character characteristics. Notwithstanding, meta-investigations have discovered that EI has generous legitimacy in any event while controlling for IQ, and character

## Chapter 1. What Is Emotional Intelligence?

Emotional intelligence (EI) alludes to the capacity to see, control and assess emotions. A few scientists recommend that emotional intelligence be learned, and strengthened, while others guarantee it's an inherent trademark.

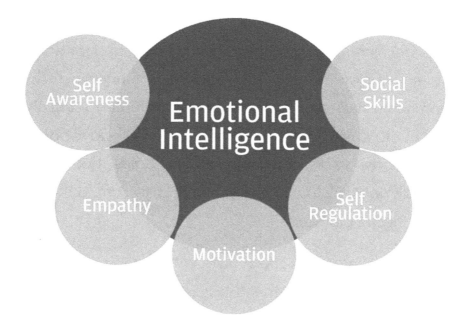

The capacity to communicate, and control emotions is fundamental, yet so can understand, decipher and react to others' feelings. Envision a world wherein you could not know when a companion was feeling tragic or when a collaborator was furious. Therapists allude to this capacity as emotional intelligence and a few specialists even recommend that it tends to be a higher priority than IQ in your general accomplishment in life.

## How Emotional Intelligence Is Measured

Different evaluations have arisen to quantify levels of emotional intelligence. For the most part, such tests can be categorized as one of two kinds: self-report tests, and capacity tests.

Self-report tests are the most well-known because they are the least demanding to manage, and score. On such tests, respondents react to questions or articulations by rating their practices. For instance, on an explanation, for example, "I regularly feel that I understand how others are feeling," a test-taker may depict the assertion as dissent, to some degree deviate, concur, or unequivocally concur.

Capacity tests, then again, include having individuals react to circumstances, and then surveying their abilities.

Such tests regularly expect individuals to exhibit their capacities, which an outsider then appraises.

If you are taking an emotional intelligence test controlled by psychological wellness proficient, here are two estimates that may be utilized:

- **Mayer-Salovey-Caruso Emotional Intelligence Test (MSCEIT)** is a capacity-based test that actions the four parts of Mayer, and Salovey's EI model. Test-takers perform assignments intended to evaluate their capacity to see, identify, understand and oversee emotions.

- **The emotional, and Social Competency Inventory (ESCI)** depends on a more seasoned instrument known as the Self-Assessment Questionnaire and includes having individuals who understand the individual offer evaluations of that individual's capacities in a few different emotional abilities. The test is intended to assess the social, and emotional capabilities that help recognize individuals as solid pioneers.

There are also many more casual online assets, a large number of them free, to explore your emotional intelligence.

## History of Emotional Intelligence

Emotional intelligence as a term didn't come into our vernacular until around 1990. Despite being a generally new term, interest in the idea has developed enormously from that point forward.

## Early Growth

As right on time as the 1930s, the analyst Edward Thorndike portrayed the idea of "social intelligence" as the capacity to coexist with others. During the 1940s, analyst David Wechsler suggested that different compelling intelligence segments could assume a significant part in how fruitful individuals are in life.

## Later Developments

The 1950s saw the ascent of the way of thinking known as humanistic brain science, and masterminds; for example, Abraham Maslow concentrated on the different ways that individuals could develop emotional fortitude.

Another significant idea to arise in the improvement of emotional intelligence was the thought of different intelligence bits. This idea was advanced during the 1970s by Howard Gardner, presenting the possibility that intelligence was something other than a solitary, general capacity.

## The Emergence of Emotional Intelligence

It was not until 1985 that the expression "emotional intelligence" was first utilized by Wayne Payne's doctoral exposition. In 1987, in an article distributed in Mensa

Magazine, Keith Beasley used the expression "emotional quotient."

In 1990, clinicians Peter Salovey, and John Mayer distributed their landmark article, "Emotional Intelligence," in the diary Imagination, Cognition and Personality. They characterized emotional intelligence as "the capacity to screen one's own, and others' sentiments, and emotions, to separate among them and to utilize this data to manage one's reasoning, and activities."

In 1995, the idea of emotional intelligence was promoted after the distribution of Daniel Goleman's book "Emotional Intelligence: Why It Can Matter More Than IQ."

## 1.1 Emotional Intelligence, and Everyday Life

There are times in life when you take a gander at somebody, and miracle, "How could she be generally so absolutely in charge of things?" Whether it is a partner who manages interesting work circumstances without annoying anyone or a companion who causes total aliens to feel good not long after gathering them. The appropriate response lies in their emotional intelligence or the capacity to screen their own emotions just like others.

You see genuine emotional intelligence instances around you consistently. You even utilize your emotional intelligence to explore ordinary circumstances and connections without acknowledging them. For example, an associate whom the manager has reprimanded should impart his sentiments to you. You listened compassionately, then equitably clarify the potential purposes behind the supervisor's annoyance and encourage your associate on the most proficient method to stay away from this later on., and you do this without disturbing or culpable your associate. This is an exemplary illustration of utilizing your emotional intelligence at work.

Consistently, endless individuals use sympathy, and understanding to handle social communications at work; for example, in an office meeting, when one individual talks, others tune in. This happens precipitously and such practices are instances of emotional intelligence in the work environment. There will consistently be a few groups who intrude on every other person, yet here we will zero in on emotional intelligence instances being utilized to improve social cooperations.

## Practical Examples Of Emotional Intelligence

We should investigate the science behind emotional intelligence. Daniel Goleman, the leading expert on emotional intelligence, broke emotional intelligence into five significant parts. They are mindfulness, self-guideline, inspiration, sympathy,, and social abilities.

Goleman indicates these five parts of emotional intelligence assume a significant role in creating a fruitful pioneer. There are different instances of pioneers utilizing their emotional quotient to control their activities.

1. Leaders rouse and are not terrified of taking intense choices pointed toward accomplishing their objectives.
2. Leaders seem to be sure, legit, direct and mindful.
3. Leaders are receptive and they dominate in correspondence.
4. Leaders are sympathetic toward others, and are also ready to impact others' feelings, and activities.

Allow us to take a gander at the everyday issues in which emotional intelligence proves to be helpful:

- Example of emotional intelligence in our everyday lives

Influential pioneers are not unmindful of their deficiencies. In any case, they have the drive to improve every day.

Had you been rugged, reluctant to acknowledge your deficiencies, or impervious to chipping away at personal development, would you genuinely end up in a good place? To turn into a fruitful pioneer, you need to create mindfulness to perceive, and beat your shortcomings.

Alternatively, would you need to contribute to the achievement of somebody who doesn't have a lot of mindfulness and is amazingly impervious to input and development ideas? This sort of individual won't develop and they are probably not going to become pioneers.

Pioneers focus on self-improvement, on obtaining new abilities and engaging others by appointing assignments, and duty. Such conduct by pioneers is an illustration of emotional intelligence in our everyday life.

## Chapter 2 The Primary, and Secondary Emotions

Having the option to feel emotions is essential for what makes us human. Numerous individuals battle to understand their feelings, and the things that cause us to feel so profoundly. Emotionally, we regularly experience a colossal scope of different items in light of any circumstance. If you are discouraged, it is a typical misinterpretation that all you feel is dismal when the truth is told; you likely think numerous things like forlorn, undetectable, irrelevant, sad and more. The large explanation numbers of us battle to identify our emotions appropriately because they are regularly gone as quick as they show up. We are continually encountering new things, which implies our emotions are once in a while static, which confuses having the option to identify what is new with our feelings.

### What Are Emotions?

Emotions come from the Latin expression more significance moving. The term is a blend of energy, and movement, which is how life is continually in streaming movement. Emotions are something we often feel and can happen when activities or sentiments mix a specific reaction inside us. We may feel emotions from a circumstance, an encounter, or from recollections. They help us understand the things we are encountering, and communicate how those things cause us to feel, whether they are fortunate or unfortunate.

In some cases, on account of injury, emotions can stall out or closed off, so when we experience them once more, we can't measure or respond appropriately to them. Positive emotions are intended to build up an encounter as pleasant, so we search it out once more. They initiate the prize systems inside the mind, which causes us to have a sense of security. Negative emotions, then again, caution us of possibly perilous circumstances, and raise the endurance impulses inside us, so we become substantially more mindful. Our feelings have developed to help us endure a more cerebral society than that of our removed predecessors. However, the responses are a lot of something very similar.

## Constructing Emotions

As indicated by HUMAINE, there are 48 perceived emotions proposed in the emotional explanation, and portrayal language. Globally, there are 128 perceived emotions, including numerous that have no name in English. Most clinicians concur with this, with the alternative to classify them further. The essential, optional and tertiary methodology was initially depicted in 1987 in the Journal of Personality, and Social Psychology as a tree shape beginning with oneself, and essential, auxiliary,, and tertiary emotions broadening like branches from the storage compartment the character.

This was the subsequent stage from Plutchik's wheel of emotions. The wheel is a lot simpler for customers to understand because it also utilizes shadings to classify both positive, and negative emotions, just as making it simpler to identify restricting emotions. This wheel was also advantageous because it was simpler to identify the different powers from a solitary feeling, and the connection between one surface, and another.

In 2012 an exploration piece dependent on Plutchik's petals confirmed that maybe therapists were too expansive in their meaning of emotions. Examination of 42 facial muscles used to make emotional reactions was simply ready to make four fundamental emotions; each different was either too comparable or a sub feeling of one of those four. For instance, the facial response to shock, and that of dread were comparative; however, this could also be because the wide-peered toward look is an endurance sense to increment visual consideration, fundamental by, and extensive that evoke dread shock.

**Primary, and Secondary**

Imagine something has occurred, anything and abruptly you are feeling a feeling. It is solid; it is the principal response to what exactly has happened. That is an essential feeling. Primary emotions are the body's first reaction and they are typically effortless to identify because they are so solid. The most widely recognized important emotions are dread, satisfaction, bitterness, and outrage.

These may also be optional emotions given different circumstances, yet when we initially respond, it's a rule with one of the abovementioned. If the telephone rang, and somebody began hollering at you for reasons unknown, you would most likely feel irate or apprehensive, or if the phone rang, and somebody revealed to you that your canine had passed on, you would feel miserable. There doesn't need to be a gigantic boost to evoke an essential feeling. Primary emotions are versatile because they cause us to respond to a specific route without being polluted or analyzed. They are a lot of an instinctual, base, endurance reaction.

## Primary Emotions

Primary emotions are more emigrating than secondary emotions, so they are less convoluted, and more apparent. We feel the main thing is straightforwardly associated with the occasion or upgrade; however, we battle to interface a similar feeling with the experience because our emotions have changed over the long haul.

## Secondary Emotions

Secondary emotions are considerably more mind-boggling because they regularly allude to the sentiments you have about the essential feeling. These are taken in emotions which we get from our parent(s) or crucial guardians as we grow up. For instance, when you feel furious, you may feel embarrassed a while later, or when you feel satisfied, you may feel alleviation or pride. In Star Wars, Master Yoda clarified optional emotions impeccably - "fear encourages outrage, outrage prompts disdain, disdain prompts languishing."

Secondary emotions can also be separated into instrumental emotions. These are oblivious, and ongoing. We learn instrumental emotions as kids as a type of molding. When we cry, a parent comes to relieve us; thus, we figure out how to utilize the outward appearances, and reactions related to calling when we need that alleviating or feeling that all is well with the world.

Numerous little children are incredibly proficient at utilizing instrumental emotions to get everything they might want with outrage. A baby pitches a fit and guardians yield to make them calm. As we get more seasoned, we discover that this conduct isn't fitting; if not, we become ruined, and manipulative. Not learning the proper optional emotional reaction leaves the individual far off, and emotionally segregated from everyone around them.

Let's investigate a portion of the fundamental kinds of emotions and investigate their effect on human conduct.

## Fear

Fear is an incredible feeling that can also assume a significant part in endurance. When you encounter a type of threat and experience fear, you go through what is known as the battle or flight reaction.

Your pulse and breath increment, your muscles become tense, and your psyche wakes up, preparing your body to one or the other run from the threat or stand, and battle.

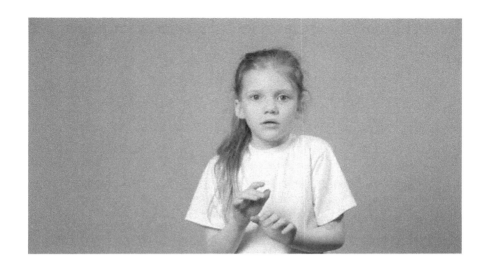

This reaction ensures that you are set up to manage dangers in your current circumstance successfully. Expressions of this kind of feeling can include:

- **Facial expressions**: like extending the eyes, and pulling back the jaw

- **Body language**: endeavors to cover up or bug from the danger

- **Physiological reactions**: like quick breathing, and heartbeat

Not every person encounters fear similarly. A few groups might be more touchy to fear and specific circumstances or articles might be bound to trigger this feeling.

Fear is the emotional reaction to an immediate danger. We can also build up a comparative response to expected risks or even our musings about possible perils, which is our opinion about tension. Social tension, for instance, includes an expected dread of social circumstances.

A few groups, then again, really search out fear inciting circumstances. Outrageous games, and different rushes can be fear prompting, yet a few groups appear to flourish, and even appreciate such emotions.

This is the thought behind openness treatment, wherein individuals are step by step presented to the things that scare them in a controlled, and safe way. In the long run, sensations of fear start to diminish.

## Sadness

Sadness is another kind of feeling frequently characterized as a transient emotional state described by sensations of disillusionment, misery, sadness, lack of engagement and a hosed mindset.

Like different emotions, bitterness is something that all individuals experience every once in a while. At times, individuals can encounter delayed, and extreme times of bitterness that can transform into melancholy. Pity can be communicated in various manners, including:

- Crying

- Dampened state of mind

- Lethargy

- Quietness

- Withdrawal from others

The sort, and seriousness of sadness can fluctuate contingent on the main driver and how individuals adapt to such sentiments can also differ.

Misery can regularly lead individuals to take part in methods for dealing with stress, for example, staying away from others, self-curing and ruminating on negative contemplations. Such practices can worsen sensations of misery and drag out the term of the feeling.

## Surprise

Surprise is another of the six essential kinds of human emotions initially depicted by Eckman. Surprise is typically very concise and is portrayed by a physiological alarm reaction following something startling.

This kind of feeling can be good, harmful, or nonpartisan. An undesirable surprise, for instance, may include somebody leaping out from behind a tree, and startling you as you stroll to your vehicle around evening time.

An illustration of a beautiful surprise would show up home to find that your dearest companions have accumulated to praise your birthday. Shock is regularly described by:

- **The Facial Expressions**: like raising the foreheads, enlarging the eyes and opening the mouth

- **The Physical Reactions**: for example, hopping back

- **The Verbal Responses**: like shouting, shouting, or panting

Surprise is another sort of feeling that can trigger the battle or flight reaction. When alarmed, individuals may encounter an explosion of adrenaline that readies the body to one or the other action or flee.

Surprise can effectively affect human conduct. For instance, research has shown that individuals will, in general, lopsidedly notice excellent occasions.

This is why significant, and surprising news events will generally stand out in memory more than others. Exploration has also discovered that individuals will be more influenced by great contentions and gain more from astonishing data.

## Happiness

Of the relative multitude of different sorts of emotions, happiness will, in general, be the one that individuals make progress toward the most. Happiness is frequently characterized as a lovely emotional expression described by sensations of satisfaction, bliss, gratification, fulfillment and prosperity.

Examination on happiness has expanded significantly since the 1960s inside various orders, including brain science known as sure brain science. This sort of feeling is some of the time communicated through:

- **The Facial Reactions**: like grinning

- **The Body language**: like a casual position

- **The Tone of voice**: a playful, excellent method of talking

While happiness is viewed as one of the basic human emotions, the things we think will make happiness will be intensely impacted by culture. For instance, mainstream society impacts will generally underline that accomplishing certain things like purchasing a home or having a lucrative occupation will bring about happiness.

The fundamental factors of what adds to happiness are frequently considerably more mind-boggling, and all the more exceptionally individualized.2 People have since quite a while ago accepted that happiness, and wellbeing were associated and research has upheld the possibility that pleasure can assume a part in both physical, and emotional well-being.

Happiness has been connected to an assortment of results, including expanded life span, and developed marital satisfaction. Conversely, unhappiness has been linked to a variety of chronic frailty results.

Stress, tension, sadness and forlornness, for instance, have been connected to things like brought down invulnerability, expanded aggravation and diminished life anticipation.

**Zest**

Zest is an emotional capability concerning strong willpower. When we put resources into zestful practices, we experience appreciation, expectation and love.

Exploring in a portion of the significant spaces of emotional well-being in the previous few years has set up zest as an essential factor for life fulfillment and the general ability to be self-aware. It is a 'heart' strength which, alongside comparative characteristics like appreciation, expectation and love, predicts an individual's happiness, and level of satisfaction from his work life, and his own life.

Feeling high-spirited and cheerful everyday conditions our mind to shape neural organizations that cause us to feel upbeat, which is why zestful individuals don't need to invest much exertion in removing inspiration – they reflect it suddenly.

And accordingly, zestful individuals are:

- Noble life partners

- Excessive performers

- High achievers

- Outstanding team workers

- Empathetic, and merciful

- Encouraging others, and themselves

- Good audience members, and communicators

## Pride

Pride is a positive emotional reaction or mentality to something with a personal association with oneself because of its apparent worth. This might be one's capacities or accomplishments, positive qualities of companions or family, or one's country.

Richard Taylor characterized pride as "the justified love of oneself" instead of bogus pride or narcissism. Additionally, St. Augustine described it as "the love of one's excellence",, and Meher Baba called it "the specific inclination through which pride manifests."

Scholars, and social clinicians have noticed that pride is a perplexing secondary feeling which requires the improvement of an ability to be self-aware, and the authority of important applied qualifications (for example, that pride is unmistakable from happiness, and euphoria) through language-based association with others. Some friendly analysts identify the nonverbal articulation of pride as a method for sending a utilitarian, consequently seeing a high social status sign. Conversely, pride could also be characterized as a modest conflict with reality.

## Optimism

Optimism is the capacity to take a gander at the brighter side of life and keep an uplifting mentality despite misfortune. Hopefulness is a marker of one's uplifting demeanor, and point of view. It includes staying confident, and robust, regardless of infrequent troubles. Idealism is something contrary to negativity, which is a typical manifestation of depression.

## Disgust

Disgust is one more of the first six fundamental emotions portrayed by Eckman. Contempt can be shown in various manners, including:

- **The Body Expression**: getting some distance from the object of disgust

- **The Physical Responses**: like regurgitating or spewing

- **The Facial reactions**: Such as wrinkling the nose, and twisting the upper lip

This feeling of repugnance can start from various things, including an unsavory taste, sight, or smell. Analysts accept that this feeling developed as a response to food sources that may be hurtful or lethal. When individuals smell or taste food sources that have turned sour, for instance, disgust is a commonplace response.

Bad cleanliness, contamination, blood, decay and demise can also trigger a disgust reaction. This might be the body's method of keeping away from things that may convey communicable diseases.7

Individuals can also encounter moral disgust when they notice others participating in practices that they discover disagreeable, indecent, or evil.

## Anger

Anger can be an incredibly fantastic feeling described by sensations of aggression, fomentation, dissatisfaction and opposition towards others. Like fear, anger can have an impact on your body's battle or flight reaction.

When a danger creates sensations of anger, you might be slanted to fight off the threat, and secure yourself. Anger is regularly shown through:

- **The Facial expressions**: like grimacing or glaring
- **The Body responses**: like taking a solid position or dismissing
- **The Tone of voice**: talking bluntly or shouting
- **The Physiological expressions**: like perspiring or becoming red
- **The Aggressive behaviors**: like hitting, kicking, or tossing objects

While anger is regularly considered a negative feeling, it can now be something worth being thankful for. It tends to be productive in explaining your necessities in a relationship and it can also persuade you to make a move, and discover answers for things that are irritating you.

Anger can turn into an issue, notwithstanding when it is inordinate or communicated in undesirable, dangerous, or hurtful manners to other people. Uncontrolled anger can rapidly go to animosity, abuse, or viciousness.

This feeling can obtain both mental, and actual results. Unchecked anger can settle on it challenging to decide on rational choices and can even affect your physical health.

Anger has been connected to coronary heart illnesses, and diabetes. It has also been linked to practices that act on well-being dangers such as aggressive driving, liquor utilization and smoking.

## Love

As indicated by Brown, emotions as occurrent mental states are "unusual substantial changes brought about by the specialist's assessment or examination of some article or circumstance that the specialist accepts to be of worry to that person." He explains this by saying that in love, we "esteem" the individual for having "a specific complex of launched characteristics" that is "open-finished" so we can keep on adoring the individual even as she changes over the long run. These characteristics, which incorporate recorded, and social factors, are assessed in love as advantageous. The entirety of this appears to explain what love's conventional article is, an errand that is central to understanding love as a feeling appropriate. Subsequently, Brown seems to say that love's traditional item is simply being beneficial (or, given his models, maybe: advantageous personally),, and he opposes being any more specific than this to safeguard the open-mindedness of love.

With love, the difficulty is to discover anything of this sort [i.e., a formal object] that is interestingly proper to love. I propose that there isn't anything of this sort that should be thus, and that this differentiates it, and disdain from different emotions.

Hamlyn proceeds to propose that love, and disdain may be early-stage emotions, a sound or negative "feeling towards," assumed by any remaining feelings.

## 2.1 Why Do We Need Emotions?

Emotions help us make a move, endure, strike and stay away from danger, decide,, and understand others. Besides, they assist others with understanding us.

From a developmental standpoint, cerebrum structures that interact with psychological data (like neocortex) are route more youthful than other mind territories that are balanced self-sufficiently (like brainstem); one could say that the impact of emotions on human conduct is a lot more noteworthy contrasted with discernment, and judicious choices.

Further, other human's emotions influence our own by temperance of the data they pass on. When we see somebody's outward appearance to reflect fear, we will, in general, split the second post for dangerous or perilous upgrades in the climate. Similarly, we feel great, and safe when detecting happiness in others. Thus, emotions, insights and conduct of people can undoubtedly be influenced by emotional upgrades.

## How can emotions be measured?

What emotions are, and how they are seen differ contingent upon numerous variables. Subsequently, getting some information about their feelings may be precarious since verbal reports are determined by familiarity with inward states, social effect and vocal capability.

One approach to evade this is to utilize physiological estimates, which are general, and more unbiased than verbal reports. Excitement, and valence, for example, can be estimated using a few psychological, social strategies like EEG, GSR, ECG, outward appearance examination, or eye following.

## The Core Emotions

The center emotions are sadness, fear, anger, bliss, fervor, sexual energy, and disgust.

Developmentally, we've built up these emotions so we can respond to our surroundings quicker than our reasoning minds can grasp. A center feeling is set off in the limbic system, in the cerebrum. Before we have any conscious control of what's going on, the limbic system is starting up the lower mind to invigorate the vagus nerve, which is the biggest nerve in the body interfacing with practically all aspects of our body., and this is how a specific feeling—suppose anger—so rapidly influences the body and sets us up for an emotional reaction to help us endure, such as warding off an assault. That is the motivation behind center emotions: to make us naturally, and rapidly create a move intended to be versatile for endurance.

The vast majority of us understand this about fear: If right now a wild bear were to bust into your home, you would run for your life before you realized that you were frightened. Your legs would begin, and you would take off. Then when you mainly were protected, and you could hinder a smidgen, you'd survey for danger. It's just by then that you would have the option to enroll that your heart was pulsating quick and that you were encountering the center feeling of fear.

What a considerable lot of us don't understand is this fundamental thought that centers emotions occur. They're not under conscious control. I don't think about you, yet I was brought up in a climate where I was informed that I had the option to control my emotions. I was required to be superior to them, more significant than them. That implied I was "together."

Be that as it may, emotions simply are. They're customized from birth to do their thing. We feel them truly. At the point when our folks do avow them as we grow up, we come to perceive: Oh, this substantial inclination in my chest—I know I'm sad. Or, on the other hand: This consuming red warmth in me is anger.

Emotions are intended to advance us toward valuable things for us and away from terrible things for us. At the point when we can run from danger, which is the thing that fear is for. When we can't run—and we need to battle since we are assaulted and offended, and we can't move away—we have anger, which is an impetus for change. Since love and association are essential to endurance, we have sadness when we experience misfortune—when we lose what we need, regardless of whether it's an association with someone else or an association with an article. When we see something we like and are keen on, we feel the energy in our bodies, and it moves us; it presents us. When we think euphoria, we feel sweeping and need to share it.

## Why are some people more sensitive or emotional than others?

A profoundly delicate individual (HSP) is a term for the individuals who are thought to have expanded or more profound focal sensory system affectability to physical, emotional, or social boosts

Is it safe to say that you are an exceptionally touchy individual? or then again. Do you know somebody in your own or expert life who is profoundly delicate?

Indeed, High affectability can be characterized as intense mental, physical and emotional reactions to the outer (social, natural) or inward (intra-individual) boost. An exceptionally delicate individual can be a self-observer, a social butterfly, or someplace in the middle.

An exceptionally touchy individual (HSP) is a term for individuals who are thought to have expanded or more profound focal sensory system affectability to physical, emotional, or social upgrades. Some allude to this as having tangible preparing affectability or SPS as a temporary structure.

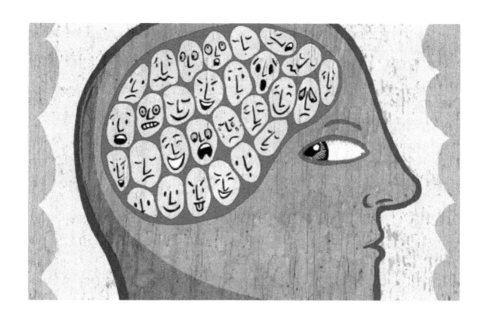

Even though there are numerous positive parts of being a delicate individual, like a more prominent capacity to tune in, and have a more noteworthy sympathy or instinct, and a better understanding of others, high affectability also antagonistically influences one's well-being, and happiness, and achievement, and frequently convolutes connections.

As indicated by Dr Sonal Anand, a Psychiatrist in Wockhardt Hospital at Mira Road, Mumbai, Being profoundly delicate can be a mix of your hereditary qualities, and the natural factors that assume a significant part. Like if you have a very peaceful parent, the odds of you getting touchy increments. It also relies upon the sort of individual you have become like the encounters you get or how you are raised and the qualities you have learned can decide the affectability in you. By the age of 17 to 18, 95% of your character is created.

"Indeed, being touchy for few things is fine, such as in regards to your accomplice or life partner or relationship, and relative as it can improve your relationship; however, here, and there being excessively delicate can prompt uneasiness issues, and melancholy. This is the most widely recognized reason for despondency; the greater part of my patients who are in discouragement frequently say that they are exceptionally delicate or easily overlooked details disturb them a ton," she said.

"If you feel that you can't handle a circumstance or you have tension, or you are into melancholy, then you should visit your specialist for help. Be that as it may, self-care, and building your certainty matter a great deal while taking treatments can help you as well. Besides, self-improvement can be incredible for you, similar to you can identify which things make you more upset and you can chip away at it," she added.

While numerous individuals may encounter a portion of these signs occasionally, a profoundly touchy individual will probably "feel excessive", and "feel excessively profound." Some people might be exceptionally delicate to only a couple of improvements, while others might be emphatically influenced by additional on the rundown.

Profoundly touchy individuals are a large portion of the occasions depicted as being "excessively delicate", and it is considered a character characteristic in individuals.

These terms were first instituted by therapists Elaine Aron, and Arthur Aron during the 1990s,, and interest in the idea has kept on developing enormously from that point forward.

Anybody could be an HSP, regardless of whether a man or lady, grown-up or kid. A high delicate individual has a more touchy focal sensory system, making them profoundly sensitive to physical, emotional, or social upgrades than others.

## Chapter 3. The Personal Competencies Of Emotional Intelligence

Your level of individual capability is one portion of building up your emotional intelligence (EQ). It comprises two key ascribes:

## Mindfulness

This is your capacity to perceive your own emotions, and their impacts on yourself, and others. It addresses EQ's establishment because it is difficult to move into the other EQ abilities such as self-administration, and social mindfulness without monitoring, and understanding your own emotions.

## Self-Management

Expands on your mindfulness, utilizing your restraint to guarantee your emotions don't control you paying little heed to the circumstance. It includes using what you think about your feelings to both deals with these emotions and rouses yourself.

Mindfulness implies that you understand how you feel and can precisely survey your emotional state. To do this, you need the accompanying abilities:

- Emotional mindfulness
- Accurate self-evaluation
- Self-certainty

Altogether, for an individual to be emotionally mindful, they may have to acknowledge that they have an inbuilt hesitance to concede to particular negative sentiments. This can be overwhelmed by monitoring the practices resulting from these negative emotions instead of essentially admitting the hidden negative feelings.

You can perceive a person who has a significant degree of emotional mindfulness since they will:

- Know which emotions they are feeling, and why
- Realize the connections between their sentiments, and their opinion, do,, and say
- Recognize what their emotions mean for their presentation
- Have directing attention to their qualities, and objectives
- Adopt practices that limit the impacts of their own emotions on a circumstance.

When you can identify your own emotions, and what they can mean for circumstances, you can precisely survey yourself. This empowers you to understand, and investigate your qualities, and shortcomings, just as being willing to explore them with others.

Daniel Goleman portrays exact self-appraisal regarding individuals who are:

- Aware of their qualities, and shortcomings
- Reflective, and equipped for gaining for a fact
- Open to candid criticism, and new points of view
- Interested in persistent learning, and self-advancement
- Able to show an awareness of what's funny, and point of view about themselves.

Self-evaluation includes genuinely examining, and recognizing your emotional qualities, and shortcomings. Considering your encounters, and characterizing critical activities needed to address any setback could help you accomplish this.

Building up a solid capacity for self-appraisal will help you gain from new encounters since it will feature those territories that offer chances for personal growth, and improvement.

The last competency of mindfulness is that of fearlessness. This is your capacity to ground yourself so you are secure, and confident in whatever circumstance you may get yourself. Daniel Goleman depicts boldness as:

'A solid feeling of one's self-esteem, and abilities.'

You will perceive people with a significant degree of fearlessness because their conduct, and correspondences show that they have a:

- Certainty about their worth, and capacities
- Strong presence
- A high degree of confidence
- Willingness to communicate a disagreeable assessment or stand okay with something correct if it is the thing that they accept
- Ability to settle on fast choices even in dubious, and compressed conditions
- Believe that they can handle the heading of their lives -, and they do.

Fearless individuals understand that they have much command over what occurs in their lives. This implies that the more self-assured you can turn into, the more you will find that you can impact your future.

When you know what your emotions mean for your conduct, and mentality towards circumstances, you will want to self-oversee. To accomplish this, you utilize your restraint to deal with your emotions, whatever your conditions and propel yourself to succeed.

By understanding, and having the option to control your emotions, you can oversee them produce positive communications with those you come into contact with. The competency of self-administration has six different ability ascribes:

**Self-control -** the capacity to stay formed whatever express your emotions are in. Individuals with this capability:

- Manage their incautious sentiments, and upsetting emotions well
- Stay formed, cheerful and unflappable even in attempting minutes

- Think plainly, and remain on track under tension

**Dependability** - implies that you will do what you say when you say you'll do it. Individuals with this capability:

- Act morally, and are unquestionably sound
- Build trust through their dependability, and authenticity
- Admit their slip-ups, and stand up to dishonest activities in others
- Take intense, principled stands regardless of whether they are disagreeable

**Good faith** - includes an individual being intensive, cautious or watchful, and infers a craving to play out an assignment well. Individuals with this fitness:

- Meet responsibilities, and keep guarantees
- Hold themselves responsible for meeting their goals
- Are coordinated, and cautious in their work

**Versatility** - the capacity to change something, or oneself, to fit happening changes. Individuals with this capability:

- Smoothly handle different demands, shifting needs and quick change
- Adapt their reactions, and strategies to fit liquid conditions
- They are adaptable by the way they see occasions

**Accomplishment direction** - requires a person to show worry for running after a willful and characterized standard of greatness. Individuals with this capability:

- Set themselves trying objectives
- Measure their presentation against those objectives
- Actively search out data to take care of business
- Use their time proficiently

**Activity** - implies starting to lead the pack in critical thinking, and compromise, just as making a move to keep issues from happening in any case. Individuals with this fitness:

- Seek out new thoughts from a wide assortment of sources
- Entertain unique answers for issues
- Generate novel thoughts
- Take new points of view, and dangers in their reasoning

**Self-administration** is essential for a supervisor because nobody needs to work for somebody who isn't in charge of themselves, and whose responses rely upon their overarching disposition.

---

## 3.1 Components Of Emotional Intelligence: Self-Awareness

Self-awareness is one of the vital segments of emotional intelligence (EI).

Daniel Goleman, the master of emotional intelligence, identified self-awareness as emotional awareness, accurate self-appraisal and self-certainty. It is tied in with knowing your emotions, your qualities, and shortcomings and having your very own solid feeling worth.

Set forth plainly, self-awareness is an understanding of your identity, the thing that your qualities and shortcomings are, how you had the chance to be that way, and how your essence and conduct influence others. (You may also track down this under "self-awareness hypothesis" in your science course reading.) To create self-awareness requires progressing work.

### Why It's Important to act naturally Aware

Self-awareness also goes hand-in-hand with emotional intelligence; individuals who are all emotionally wise regularly have more significant self-awareness levels.

Maybe more significantly, acting naturally aware and understanding emotions are two qualities that numerous businesses search for while recruiting and advancing.

Anyway, you might be asking yourself, what are self-awareness abilities? and how would I turn out to be more self-aware?

Here are a few signs that you have some work to do, and that you may not be pretty much as self-aware as you might suspect you are—and what to do about it.

Attributes of individuals who are not self-aware

## 1. You micromanage.

Nearly any individual who micromanages has a valid justification concerning why they do it. Maybe you're a stickler. Perhaps there's a great deal riding on a specific venture and you can't allow it to get away from your consideration. Or on the other hand, perhaps you understand that your colleague needs an additional push to finish tasks or an undertaking.

These are, for the most part, legitimate reasons. Be that as it may, you understand what's absent from them? An understanding of what you're craving to take control means for the other individual. Micromanaging effects affect laborers, colleagues, and individuals as a rule. It signals you don't believe the individuals you're working with. It also allows you to make a ton of presumptions, serving to avoid your duty to set aside the effort to accomplish the work, and impart.

Work on confiding in others. You don't exist in a vacuum; others are working with you toward a similar objective. Figuring out how to appoint, and perceive others can do the work, and shows development, and development.

## 2. Nothing is ever your shortcoming.

Talking about keeping away from obligation, how frequently do you wind up saying, "Indeed, however, it's not my deficiency since (embed reason/pardon/setting here)?"

It's common to need to offer setting to a circumstance, particularly if you feel assaulted or if something indeed wasn't your issue. If you consistently react to input or studies with "certainly, yet... ", you're in all likelihood attempting to divert undesirable negative consideration. That is understandable. However, realize that others see you as cavalier, and as an individual who keeps away from responsibility.

Having the awareness to perceive how individuals respond to your sentiments' appearance is a vital working environment ability. It's right up there with emotional intelligence; you should have the option to isolate your musings with an accurate perception of your partners' conduct. At the point when you commit an error, assume liability for it. Partners, and administrators are bound to react emphatically to somebody who recognizes the mix-up and apologizes than somebody who continually dodges fault.

### 3. You get protective.

Does any input will in general, drive you furious or crazy? Do you discover all information is unforgiving, startling, or unjustifiable? At whatever point an associate offers analysis, do negative emotions winding crazy?

If you addressed yes to any of these inquiries, you should check in with yourself concerning why you get vexed. After you're finished with your thoughtfulness and you have the appropriate response, wonder why once more.

Input, and studies are a piece of life — particularly busy working — and is frequently intended to help you develop. Since no one is awesome and I say this with sympathy, not all things are about you. It's not generally close to home.

It very well may be challenging to sit with distress. While it's entirely expected to feel restless or annoyed with startling analysis, it's critical to understand, and identify how it differs from justified, and target input. Utilize the following information you get as a self-awareness exercise to help you further create self-awareness at work.

### 4. You make statements you don't mean.

There are times when I wish individuals could guess what I might be thinking — that they'd naturally know when, and why I am vexed or disappointed or hurt. It would make life such a ton simpler than being a grown-up and express my emotions.

It's also simpler —, and emotionally more secure — to react with "nothing" or "no issue" when something is, indeed, an issue. When difficult situations arise, we will, in general, cover our emotions.

It bodes well—we as a whole need to seem able, and sure to individuals, mainly grinding away. Detached forceful conduct is an approach to keep away from the encounter and divert sentiments. It's frightening to be defenseless, and it tends to be especially scary at work given the wide range of various elements ladies need to explore.

If you depend on passive-aggressive conduct to impart, you're also setting unreasonable assumptions on others since people are not, indeed, telepaths. It's also debilitating — both for you, and whoever else is included.

At the point when somebody asks you how to can something or needs to say whether you're disturbed, take a beat before reacting. While it could be enticing to keep your issues inside, consider an ideal approach to outline your concern such that it communicates what you need to say without being harmful. This is a sensitive equilibrium—you most likely can't know all that you need to say, yet you also need to address the contention. If you can, plan out some arguments ahead of time, considering what you need to get across without being harmful.

## 5. You can't laugh at yourself.

I won't be humiliated, and struggle managing disgrace. (Doesn't everybody?) It's understandable that when you wind up in a circumstance where you're feeling terrible, the exact opposite thing you need to do is giggle. Perhaps you respond by blowing up and lashing out at whoever is near.

You're genuinely doing there is redirecting — as opposed to sitting with profound uneasiness, you divert yourself.

Self-awareness is the present circumstance conceding to yourself you're humiliated/disturbed/embarrassed. After that occurs, the giggling follows typically.

## 6. You believe you're a good listener.

Perhaps you indeed are a decent audience! If you think you are, it merits wondering why — what do you do that makes you one?

Have you at any point completed an undertaking, and been anxious about it? There were different pieces you needed to incorporate; however, you used up all available time, or there was this one other territory you thought could be more grounded —, and then everything except one individual gave you specific input. Who did you tune in to?

If you're in any way similar to me, you harped on the one individual who — out of the relative multitude of pioneers — affirmed your weaknesses. How regularly do you do this? What about when somebody is talking? Is it accurate to say that you are simply sitting tight for him/her to complete so you can say what you need to say? Would you be able to escape your particular manner, and focus on what the other individual is saying?

Listening is critical when conveying. That is not a mystery. But on the other hand, it isn't so essential. It's how you tune in, and what you tune in for that accurate tallies. Self-awareness incorporates the capacity to tune in as opposed to tuning in for. Consider what everybody is saying, and all that they're saying—not simply the parts that are praises or abuses.

By the day's end, anybody can get self-aware. It doesn't take a better than expected intelligence; it simply requires consideration, and contemplation. It is tuning in, tolerating criticism, sharpening your relational abilities and being genuine with yourself. Others are vital to becoming more self-aware, and eventually a superior specialist, director, companion, accomplice,, and comrade.

### Is it awful to be excessively self-aware?

Here, and there, being too self-aware can be a two-sided deal.

As indicated by research led by clinician Erika Carlson of the University of Toronto Mississauga, self-aware individuals are less inclined to react emphatically to realizing how individuals are deciphering them, and their imperfections. It is an awkward inclination to perceive how others see you—mainly when it's not in a positive light and being excessively self-aware can prompt negative sentiments about oneself, particularly thinking about the barely recognizable difference between self-awareness, and self-analysis.

Overall, while self-awareness is, for the most part, sure, it's imperative to utilize it for great, not abhorrent. Maybe then zeroing in on what's up with yourself, use your awareness to improve your connections and correspondence with others, and how you can help both yourself and individuals around you.

## Observing Yourself

We will, in general, work on "programmed pilot," as though we have no control. Actually, except if we understand what we are doing, we have minimal possibility of evolving it—and frequently, the primary demonstration of turning out to be aware makes us accomplish something different.

When we practice self-perception—seeing our opinion, feeling, doing, and envisioning—permits us to get self-aware. When we know about the thing we are doing, we understand that we have options, and decisions make us unique.

The actual demonstration of seeing how we feel can permit us to deliver or let go of a stuck or stale inclination or a self-undermining propensity. I once worked with an understudy who denied all that she was blamed for by companions, instructors, and folks. One day I said, "I need you just to notice yourself, and simply notice that you deny what you do." obviously, her prompt reaction was, "I don't." To which I giggled and said, "Notice what you just did!" I guaranteed her that this was not a task to change what she did or even adjudicator what she did, yet justifying what she did. Her errand was to become cognizant, so she knew about, and picking her conduct instead of working unknowingly. I can't say what she did away from me, yet I never heard her deny her behavior again from that day on. Simply the demonstration of awareness delivered her from the propensity.

The more perceptive we are, the more we understand the difference between the noticed, and the onlooker.

## Level Up your Mindset

I'm a solid adherent that achievement, and happiness are about the outlook. Your mentality, and conviction system influence everything in your life, from your opinion, and feel to how you act, and respond to your general surroundings.

To accomplish your objectives, your mentality needs to coordinate with your yearnings; else, it very well may be keeping you away from getting where you need to be.

Here are seven compelling ways you can overhaul your mentality:

## 1. Change your Self-Talk

The discussions you have with yourself are an immediate impression of your attitude. If you are advising yourself, "I'm not sufficient to accomplish my fantasies," your considerations will make your existence, and your outlook will keep you away from having the life you need. To update your attitude, change your negative self-converse with a strengthening discourse. Sounds buzzword, however advising yourself "I can do this" or "I got this" truly works.

## 2. Change your Language

In the wake of changing your inward idea discourse, and the story, you are advising yourself, change how you converse with others. Stay away from phrases like "I'm generally similar to this" or "I'm continually doing this" for empowering a development outlook. Moreover, make it a propensity to discuss the things working out in a good way in your life instead of griping and discussing your issues. This will energize an attitude of bounty rather than fear and need.

## 3. Decide the attitude you need, and go about as though

Pick an objective you need to accomplish and ask yourself: "Which attitude do I have to accomplish this objective?", and "Which outlook do individuals have that were fruitful at this objective?".

For instance, sound and fit individuals may share the outlook "I love dealing with my body, supporting it with entire food sources, and practicing each day.". If it's your objective to be sound and fit, go about as though you as of now HAVE the attitude of a solid and healthy individual. You are essentially deceiving your cerebrum to receive another perspective and building up to it with activity along these lines.

## 4. Learn and Apply

Guess books from incredible thoughts to understand and embrace their reasoning. Guess books about how the thoughts and mind function. Gain from outlook specialists through online courses, occasions, and instructing.

## 5. Encircle yourself with individuals that match your ideal outlook

Need to redesign your cash and achievement outlook? Begin spending time with exceptionally fruitful individuals and appear to have a wealth of money streaming their way whenever. It is simpler to embrace another mentality when you see that it is working for others. Figure out how they think and adjust their day-by-day propensities to coordinate with their mentality.

## 6. Make new propensities to help your outlook change

Incorporate excellent propensities into your day that help your attitude change and reinforce your intuition with activity. If you are overhauling from a "fixed" to "development" outlook, plan time for learning, and begin taking note of your education and accomplishments consistently. If you are updating from "objective" to "venture" attitude, work on being careful, appreciating the current second, and praising little victories.

## 7. Leap out of your usual range of familiarity

If you put yourself in circumstances that challenge you, you have no other decision than to adapt to the situation and overhaul your attitude. It turns into a need to endure.

## Forgive Yourself, and Let's Move on

A large number of us realize that pardoning is something worth being thankful for, correct? It liberates us from harshness, and anger, two emotions that don't feel better, and can disturb our actual wellbeing, and keep us away from all the great we may accomplish, and encounter. I know a considerable lot of you have chipped away at excusing others. However, what might be said about forgiving ourselves?

Regardless of whether we've gotten tremendous, and reliable about offering to pardon to other people, isn't excusing ourselves regularly the most difficult? Understanding why self-absolution is difficult can give us signs to make it simpler:

"God may excuse your wrongdoings. However, your sensory system will not." — Alfred Korzybski

At the point when we've accomplished something "incorrectly," we register it in our sensory system. A physical issue to another person may be joined by blame. A slip-up that costs us something we need may have sadness appended to it. At the point when we've accomplished something we lament, we frequently interface it to a restricting conviction like, "I'm continually expressing some unacceptable things" or "I'll always be unable to cover my bills."

If we attempt to excuse ourselves for something without delivering the hidden feeling or conviction we've joined to it, the pardoning doesn't take. Regardless of how diligently you attempt to pardon, you keep on thrashing yourself for whatever occurred—because your sensory system advises you to. What would you be able to do about that? Identify the restricting conviction or negative feeling you've appended to what exactly you're attempting to pardon in yourself. Delivery that first, utilizing an interaction like Mental Emotional Release® and you'll see that easy-going yourself isn't so difficult.

**"Absolution implies relinquishing the past." — Gerald Jampolsky**

We will, in general, consider ourselves a continuum—a person that starts with our past moves momentarily through our present, and heads toward our future. Relinquishing our past—or the previous we have made in our minds—can feel flimsy and "ungrounded," like a boat that has slipped its securing.

**"One pardons to the extent that one loves." — Francois de La Rochefoucauld**

When you truly love somebody, isn't it simpler to pardon them? If you have a trusting, adoring relationship, and your companion or significant different accomplishes something that harms you, aren't you bound to consider that to be a one-time occasion? Don't you allude back to the decency you love in them?

A ton of us doesn't have that adoring, confiding in a relationship with ourselves. A considerable lot of us are substantially more condemning of ourselves than we are of others. We'll assume the best about others; however, we will not cut ourselves any leeway whatsoever.

At the point when you're managing an individual you don't trust or like, frequently you can decide to excuse, discharge the hurt and not keep in touch with them any longer. With yourself? It is anything but a choice. You will not stop, separation or leave yourself if you don't love, and like yourself; in one way or another, you need to get your relationship with you to be surer.

## How Mindfulness Breeds Emotional Intelligence

As indicated by Peerayuth Charoensukmongkol in his book, General Self-Efficacy and Perceived Stress, care contemplation helps manifest emotional intelligence in three significant way:

4. It improves your capacity to grasp your own emotions.
5. It assists you with figuring out how to perceive the emotions of others around you.
6. It strengthens your capacity to administer and control your emotions.

He also notes that care improves an individual's capacity to utilize their emotions viably because it helps them figure out which emotions are valuable for specific exercises.

Positive emotions may be necessary for numerous situations. Anyway, there are a few circumstances where negative emotions are more dependable (2014).

If you have certain errands you need to perform, using care strategies can help you move toward an undertaking with the correct attitude.

---

# Chapter 4. Component Of Emotional Intelligence:

## 4.1 Self-Regulation

This is the capacity to control one's driving forces, the ability to think before you respond, and the power to communicate suitably. Goleman characterizes emotional development in this part as having the option to assume liability for your activities, having the opportunity to adjust to change, and the capacity to respond suitably to different people groups silly emotions or conduct.

Example: If somebody is shouting at you, you realize that they are not generally furious at you. You can understand they might resent a specific circumstance and feel they need to take it out on somebody. You don't think about this literally or respond sore back.

## Characterize your values

They influence our decisions and can say a ton regarding ourselves. Albeit not every person knows about their qualities, they are consistently present in life and become apparent in our mentality to our general surroundings and conduct even with different regular circumstances.

For what reason is information on your qualities so helpful?

Life fulfillment relies upon the uprightness of our day-by-day decisions with our qualities.

If you live as per your fundamental beliefs, you feel satisfaction and fulfillment. You experience the specific life you truly need.

When you are regularly compelled to act against your qualities, you will feel an interior struggle. It can give you a feeling that you are not simply the best form.

**Taking liability for your actions**

We are all doing what we trust it requires to be fruitful, to be our best, to have an effect and to deal with our duties. In any case, when life appears with issues, curves and snags that stand in our direction, it very well may not be difficult to lose our fervor, drive and inspiration to continue to improve.

It's frustrating when progress slows down or stops. It happens to potentially anyone. Nobody is invulnerable.

That is the point at which we need to keep an eye out that we don't stall out in the "pardon trap." This is a hazardous mental cycle that numerous individuals inadvertently, and frequently subliminally turn on in their brains.

We as a whole need to deal with the pardon of time to escape the pardon trap unequivocally. To be accountable for your consideration, and energy, you must have steps to help you take obligation regarding your time.

Here are some straightforward strides to take duty regarding your time, and your life.

## 1. Don't Blame Others

At the point when you're too caught up with pointing fingers at others, it gets difficult to see your issues. Indeed, even in circumstances where you're the person in question, accusing others doesn't get you far. All things being equal, it causes disdain, sharpness and negative energy to wait.

When you quit accusing, and acknowledge obligation, you're not, at this point, the person in question. You'll then have the advantage and have the option to change the circumstance as you would prefer.

## 2. Don't Complain

Similar to accusing others, griping doesn't go anyplace. It torments your considerations with negative energy, and, accordingly, frees you of the capacity to take care of issues.

At the point when you quit griping, you're reworking your mind to intuition all the more decidedly. You'll then have the option to zero in on every one of the things you can do to make things direct instead of harping on what turned out badly.

## 3. Change Your Perspective

One approach to assume liability is to change your emotional reaction, and association with an occasion. When I was terminated from my first work, I felt angry, and figured I didn't have the right to be given up because my manager couldn't have cared less about me. If I had instead recognized that my manager saw I was despondent at the specific employment, and that he was delivering me to get a new line of work that was more satisfying because he often thought about me, then I would have felt appreciative, and better about my subsequent stages.

## 4. Own Your Mistakes

I have met many refined, practical and exceptional change-creators on the planet, and have seen that they share one attribute – incredible individuals are not hesitant to concede they are incorrect,, and they ensure they don't rehash similar missteps twice. Extraordinary pioneers fill according to their supporters and when they apologize, and ensure they do things any other way or not in the least, later on, this conduct makes their devotees consider them to be solid individuals, and pioneers who assume liability for their mix-ups, and gain from them.

## 5. Tolerating Responsibility

Assuming liability can be humiliating, lowering, complex and even exorbitant. Be that as it may, tolerating duty regarding your decisions can also be very engaging. Assuming individual liability implies not censuring others for your unhappiness. It means that you've sorted out ways to cheerful, notwithstanding others' (harmful) practices, and external conditions.

---

## 4.2 The Motivation

This is having an interest in learning and self-improvement. It has the solidarity to continue to go when there are snags in life. It is defining objectives and finishing them. Goleman would characterize an emotionally developed individual in this class to have characteristics such as having activity, the obligation to complete an undertaking, and having determination even with difficulty.

Example: One who picks inside inspiration-driven objectives rather than outside stimulation-driven objectives. Inner inspiration-driven objectives are things, for example, acquiring a professional education or turning into a better individual; things that show self-improvement. Outside inspiration-driven objectives are things that parade riches or status. This is defining objectives, for example, having the following freshest and most pleasant vehicle.

Example: If an understudy bombs a class, they consider this a chance to learn and retake the class without self-uncertainty. They don't allow the inability to impede their objective.

The feeling is the establishment of inventiveness, enthusiasm, confidence, drive, and change. Inspiration is equivalent to energy, activity, and industriousness. An inspirational mentality in Social measurement is inspiration, one of the vital features of emotional intelligence and administration.

An idea without feeling crashes and burns; it is feeling joined to the springboard's possibility, the energy required for activity. Without emotions, whatever work we do likely would be done mechanically, influencing the whole association, including business connections. Inspiration—inner energy that moves outward one way—is a quality that recognizes the great chief from the extraordinary one. However, where does such inspiration come from?

## The Importance of Meaning

Significantly, we append importance to what we do because it will be challenging to support our inspiration or energy. Without it, when was simply the last time you requested the genuine reason for your work? Past gathering the current year's business objectives, that is, or cutting the spending plan by another 10% or arriving at net incomes of $50 million or scoring an individual monetary upset. What does everything mean? A pioneer who isn't focused on the association's motivation and who doesn't truly accept that the design is some way or another significant to society won't ever have the option to move others.

Inspiration isn't something "out there" that pushes us. We feel an external pressing factor when others ask us to do, be, or accomplish something; however, permitting our lives to be formed by facades exhausts our inventiveness and energy and is difficult to support in the long haul. Inspiration depends on a highly profound degree of what we need—an inward power that we would then be able to center toward the rest of the world. Individuals who need excitement have permitted themselves to get so got up to speed in facades that they have put some distance between that inner fire. We can do most things that we genuinely need to do! At the point when we understand our motivation and see that it gives our lives meaning, we are roused and strengthened with an inside guided responsibility that dominates outside pressure. Inspiration makes a big difference for the flames!

## Characterizing Your Purpose

When was the last time you spent quality, intelligent time considering what you truly need? The majority of us get so gotten up to speed in subtleties and exercises that we put some distance between the entirety of our energy. Enthusiasm comes from the emotional cerebrum, and when we put some distance between our most profound longings—our interests—we remove our sentiments and endanger our wellbeing. If our deep cravings don't guide our action, we won't gather up the inspiration to seek after that action. If we disregard what we profoundly want for our lives, we are, as it were, being false to ourselves. Neglecting to perceive who we indeed are inside will keep us from securing Emotional Intelligence, risk our actual wellbeing (the body-mind association), and, to top it all off—hold us back from accomplishing genuine happiness.

When we are feeling delighted with our lives, we are most likely on the correct way. Fulfillment is only a milder type of enthusiasm or inspiration. We need the break that fulfillment brings because we can't support exceptional inspiration uncertainly without resting and refocusing. Indeed, even in our less enthusiastic minutes, the power of significance and object is as yet apparent inside us and serves to control our activities.

Reconnecting with your motivation is an excellent method to reestablish energy and inspiration in your life. How severely do you need something? Is it true that you are propelled? If you don't have much eagerness, then you have not taken advantage of that inward wellspring of significance—what you genuinely appreciate and what's genuinely generally imperative to you. This is the thing that will get you energetic and spurred. Dive in your heart to find that flash of energy that will light your inward fire.

---

## 4.3 The Social Competencies Of Emotional Intelligence

In emotional intelligence, the term 'social abilities' alludes to the skills expected to adequately handle and impact others' emotions.

This may seem like control, yet it can really be just about as straightforward as understanding that grinning at individuals makes them smile back and can consequently cause them to feel considerably better.

The term 'social abilities' covers a broad scope of powers.

Social abilities, in the Emotional Intelligence sense, include:

- Persuasion, and Influencing Skills
- Communication Skills
- Conflict Management Skills
- Leadership Skills
- Change Management Skills

**Influence and Persuasion Skills**

Influence is the specialty of enthusing others and prevailing upon them to your thoughts or proposed game-plan.

Individuals who are influential or who impact read the emotional flows in a circumstance and tweak what they are saying to engage those included.

## Communication Skills

Communication abilities are indispensable to acceptable emotional intelligence. You should have the option to tune in to other people, pass on your contemplations, and, maybe more critically, sentiments.

Great communicators:

- Listen well to everyone around them, ensuring that they understand what is said, and look for full and open sharing of data. For additional, see our pages on Listening Skills, Reflection, and Clarifying.
- They are set up to catch wind of issues and don't simply need to be told about uplifting news.
- Manage complex issues straight away, and don't permit issues to putrefy.

- Register, and follow up on emotional signals in imparting, ensuring that their message is fitting.

## Conflict Management Skills

Clashes and conflicts can emerge whenever regularly appearing to show up out of nowhere.

The craft of overseeing and settling struggle is critical both at home and at work. It begins by monitoring the significance of thoughtfulness and tact and how they can assist with stopping difficult circumstances.

Great peace promoters can carry conflicts out from the dark and resolve them. They utilize sharing of emotions to empower discussion, open conversation, decrease the secret flows, and issues, and assist each gathering with perceiving each other's sentiments just like a legitimate position. They also attempt to get mutual benefit arrangements (see our Transactional Analysis and Negotiation Skills for additional).

## Leadership Skills

It might sound awkward to unite authority abilities as a feature of social skills. Emotional intelligence is essential for authority, not the alternate route around?

The appropriate response is that initiative ability and emotional intelligence are inseparably connected. As we noted before, just the fixed individuals on their own and others' emotions can impact. Maybe the vital part of good administration is impact and having the option to take others alongside you. A few group calls that allure it is more significant than that: it is acceptable emotional intelligence.

Great pioneers will:

- Have the option to verbalize a dream and enthuse others with it.
- Not should be in a conventional influential position to give authority.
- Backing and guide the exhibition of partners while considering them responsible, and
- Show others how it's done.

## Change Management Skills

Viable change directors, regularly known as change impetuses, are the individuals who get change going without distancing everybody included.

We would all understand that change usually is very unpleasant for each one of those included. Great change impetuses, notwithstanding, create an energizing open door as opposed to danger. Freely, they perceive the requirement for change and eliminate hindrances. They rock the boat and champion change. They also lead from the front, displaying the ideal shift.

## 4.4 Components Of Emotional Intelligence: Empathy

This is the capacity to understand different people group's emotions and responses. Sympathy must be accomplished if self-awareness is achieved. Goleman accepts that one should have the option to understand themselves before they can understand others. Emotional development in this classification incorporates individuals having attributes like an impression of others, being keen on different people groups stresses, and concerns, the capacity to expect someone's emotional reaction to an issue or circumstance, and the understanding of social orders standards, and why individuals act how they do.

Example: Being ready to understand adapt to somebody else difficulties or sadness. When you know yourself entirely, and why you feel the things you believe, you can understand different people groups regardless of whether they are different.

## Types of empathy

There are different sorts of compassion that analysts have characterized. These are intellectual, emotional, and caring compassion.

## Psychological Empathy

Psychological compassion, also known as 'point of view taking,' isn't actually what the more significant part of us would consider as sympathy by any means.

Psychological sympathy fundamentally has the option to place yourself into another person's place and see their viewpoint.

It is valuable expertise, especially in arrangements for instance, or for supervisors. It empowers you to imagine another person's perspective, however without fundamentally captivating with their emotions. It doesn't, in any case, genuinely fit with the meaning of sympathy as 'feeling with', being a significantly more levelheaded, and coherent interaction.

Adequately, intellectual sympathy is 'compassion by thought', as opposed to by feeling.

**Emotional Empathy**

Emotional compassion is the point at which you feel the other individual's emotions close by them, as though you had 'got' the feelings.

Emotional sympathy is also known as 'individual misery's or 'emotional disease.' This is nearer to the common understanding of the word 'compassion,' however more emotional.

Emotional sympathy is most likely the principal sort of compassion that many of us feel as youngsters. It tends to be seen when a mother grins at her infant and the infant 'gets' her feeling and smiles back. Less joyfully, maybe, an infant will regularly begin to cry if the individual hears another child crying.

## Compassionate Empathy

At last, humane sympathy is what we generally understand by compassion: sympathizing with somebody's agony and making a move to help.

The name, sympathetic sympathy, is predictable with what we as a rule understand by empathy. Like compassion, heart is tied in with feeling worry for somebody, however with an extra move towards activity to relieve the issue.

Sympathetic compassion is the sort of sympathy that is generally fitting.

When in doubt, individuals who need or need your sympathy don't simply require you to understand (psychological compassion),, and they unquestionably needn't bother with you just to sympathize with their tormentor, more regrettable, to begin crying uncontrollably close by them (emotional compassion).

All things being equal, they need you to understand, and identify with what they are going through, and, significantly, either take, or assist them with taking, activity to determine the issue, which is caring sympathy.

## How to develop empathy

Sympathy is the capacity to understand, and share someone else's sentiments, and emotions. It is vital for building great connections, both at work, and in your own life. Individuals who don't display compassion are seen as cold, and self-ingested and they frequently have separated existences. Sociopaths are broadly ailing in sympathy. Then again, somebody who is compassionate is seen as warm, and mindful.

The examination shows that sympathy is mostly inborn, and somewhat educated. Everybody can improve, nonetheless. Here are eight different ways to strengthen your own compassion:

1. **Challenge yourself.** Embrace testing encounters which push you outside your usual range of familiarity. For instance, get familiar with another expertise, like an

instrument, leisure activity, or unknown dialect. Build up another expert competency. Doing things like this will humble you and lowliness is a crucial empowering agent of sympathy.

**2. Escape your typical environment.** Travel, particularly to new places, and societies. It gives you a special appreciation for other people.

**3. Get feedback.** Request criticism about your relationship abilities (e.g., tuning in) from family, companions and associates—and then check in with them intermittently to perceive how you're doing.

**4. Investigate the heart not simply the head.** Peruse writing that investigates individual connections, and emotions. This has been appeared to improve the sympathy of youthful specialists.

**5. Stroll from others' perspectives**. Converse with others about what it resembles to stroll from their perspective—about their issues, concerns, and how they saw the encounters you both shared.

**6. Analyze your predispositions.** We as a whole have covered up (and now, and again not-so-covered up) predispositions that meddle with our capacity to tune in and sympathize. These are frequently based on obvious factors like age, race and sexual orientation. Try not to think you have any predispositions? Reconsider—we as a whole do.

**7. Develop your feeling of interest.** What would you be able to gain from an extremely youthful associate who is "unpracticed?" What would you be able to gain from a customer you see as "restricted"? Inquisitive individuals pose heaps of inquiries (point 8), driving them to build up a more grounded understanding of individuals around them.

**8. Pose better inquiries**. Bring three or four innovative, even provocative inquiries to each discussion you have with customers or associates.

Figure out how to empathize, and Build the Relationships that Truly Matter to Career Success

---

## Chapter 5. Understanding the Emotional Drain

We've all heard it. We've most likely completely said it. "I'm simply emotionally depleted today!" Rarely, notwithstanding, do we contemplate where this expression comes from or exactly how strict these manifestations and sensations may be.

As indicated by Healthline, emotional weariness is a condition of being seriously emotionally depleted or drained from the development of stress from either your work or individual life or both.

This term can also be utilized to depict "wear out" and the impression of basically shuffling excessively and feeling the impacts of an absence of energy to proceed.

At the point when we consider how quick-moving our way of life and society is, it is anything but a major surprise that we could throughout succumb to these indications and sicknesses.

We see these indications promptly in excessively demanding positions, regardless of whether in workplaces or in difficult work. In any case, emotional fatigue can spring from any horde of occupations, from nurturing to inventive work to business.

Nobody is excluded from feeling emotionally drained, yet there are approaches to seeing it coming and arm yourself against it.

The following are a few indications of feeling emotionally depleted, and how you can deal with assistance yourself and your loved ones.

## 1. Feeling "Stuck" or "Caught" in Life or a Particular Situation

When we're feeling emotionally depleted, we struggle to change and widen our view of some random circumstance. If we're battling or attempting to discover an exit from a task, relationship, or issue, not inclination emotionally solid can go about as a solid hindrance from making and keeping a new, inspirational viewpoint.

Sooner or later, we all will feel stuck in an issue in life; this turns into an indication of emotional seepage when you begin to feel like you are characteristically stuck inside the present circumstance, with no energy or way out.

This can also manifest as an absence of inspiration to search out new arrangements or an inclination that we've made plans to walk through our issues and essentially acknowledge that things won't improve.

Thus, we may create discouragement, anger, and fractiousness, which can manifest as actual diseases, like migraines, actual weakness, muscle touchiness, absence of rest, and helpless craving.

**The Solution**

One method of getting past this indication of feeling emotionally depleted is to search for help. This can be as a dear companion or relative, or it might introduce itself as expert assistance, like a specialist, specialist, or elective medication healer.

On numerous occasions, when we are feeling stuck and caught in life, we struggle to haul ourselves out of that consistent, negative circle that our brain plays through. This is truly where the advantage of the local area can become an integral factor.

Searching out help not just reduces the weight of feeling, and go through this issue alone, yet it also permits you to get info, and viewpoint from an outside, unbiased source that could be the advancement you need.

Others can gigantically affect how our issues introduce themselves, showing us an elective arrangement, we couldn't ever have thought of or found all alone.

## 2. Absence of Motivation to Work, Create and Pursue Goals, and Dreams

A lot of worries can consume even the most euphoric of plans and activities. It causes us to feel like, regardless of how enthusiastically we attempt, there is sufficiently not emotional or fiery bandwidth to do anything by any means.

This demeanor, and these psychological, and emotional states can make it exceptionally difficult for us to complete work, appreciate the way toward making something, or tackle objectives, and plans that we've invested in.

On an actual level, stress and the absence of inspiration can interfere with our energy levels to where we're feeling weariness, drowsiness, and an absence of hunger.

We may feel sluggish during all times of the day and show an unmistakable lack of engagement in performing or being beneficial. We may also show a lack of concern towards the things that typically bring us happiness, such as making arrangements with companions or dealing with our physical, mental, and emotional wellbeing.

**The Solution**

One method of re-invigorating ourselves when we do feel an absence of inspiration is to begin to get clear on why we're deficient with regards to it in any case.

Perhaps this is because we're extending ourselves excessively meager and our daily agendas have gotten genuinely overpowering. If this is the situation, maybe we can investigate focusing on our work by what is the most basic and handling those undertakings first.

Another explanation might be that you're falling into the "Accommodating person" hare opening. This is the place where you're submitting your time and energy to completing things for every other person, without checking in with yourself first.

Will you really handle that task or satisfy that guarantee? Would you even like to? These are significant inquiries to pose and speak the truth about the appropriate responses!

When you make these strides, you can re-change and rethink where you need to invest your time and exertion, subsequently kicking up your emotional energy once more.

## 3. Peevishness and "Going off the wall crazy."

When our emotions aren't in line, we make some harder memories controlling what might be seen as silly anger or abrupt upheavals. In actuality, when we're in the main part of that "wear out" sensation, we're frantically attempting to keep our cool and hold our work and undertakings back from self-destructing. It's debilitating, exhausting, and simply disappointing!

At these times, when our emotions are seared, and frantic for a reset, it's simpler for us to surrender to anger or crabbiness or to unexpected upheavals of fierceness. Emotional consumption simply searches for an exit and it doesn't mind who gets its brunt. We may feel remorseful later, yet at the time, we've lost the capacity to take a look at ourselves.

**The Solution**

One amazing method of dissolving that anger is through breath. At the point when we're angry and baffled, our breathing and heartbeat animate, all prompting enactment of the battle or flight reaction in our systems. When that kicks in, it's harder for us to think judiciously or settle on trustworthy choices. Rather than acting, we RE-act, and not generally in an ideal way.

At the point when we tap once again into our breathing, we permit it to alleviate and reset that battle or flight reaction, so the body can return to homeostasis.

**4. Continual Fatigue and Poor Sleep**

Some may believe that feeling emotionally depleted would take care of you immediately. However, the inverse is really the situation. Sleep deprivation has been connected to an unpredictable number of emotional and mental problems, and on the grounds that everything in the body-mind-soul association is complicatedly connected, it is anything but a surprise that if one thing is off, the whole system is influenced.

Getting sufficient rest is monstrously critical to the wellbeing of your general existence. Without it, we're basically running on void, and exhausting the body of what's as of now a depleting exertion.

Notice your rest examples and focus if you're struggling to relinquish the day or your daily agenda before you head to bed. Is it true that you are working over incomplete errands while attempting to nod off? Is it accurate to say that you are doing combating emotions and musings around evening time?

These all may highlight being emotionally depleted, which conveys into the following day, with steady weakness all through your day, and week.

## The Solution

One method of checking in and mitigating these manifestations is to begin making a custom rest schedule. A couple of hours before sleep time, begin to unwind any utilization of hardware or work. Whatever wasn't done that day, write it down to begin the first thing, yet begin to cut binds with it before you plan for sleep time.

This will guarantee that you're not scavenging around in your brain for some other thoughts or work when you should be giving your psyche and body truly the necessary rest.

If it helps, begin carrying out some fundamental oils to slip you into rest. Lavender, eucalyptus, and peppermint are truly alleviating, and can even assist with sinus issues or clog.

## The Final Thoughts

Emotional weariness or feeling emotionally depleted is a side-effect of something in our regular daily existence that is skewed – be it work, play, family, or anything in the middle. It's vital to thin down the main driver and rethink how you invest your energy, how you focus on your work, and how you treat your brain body-soul association for ideal prosperity.

---

## Chapter 6. The Role of Emotional Intelligence in Mental Health

The inclusion of emotional wellness has expanded in both mainstream press and scholarly exploration. There is no uncertainty that emotional wellness is on the increment and may arrive at extents that will extend administrations. While there has been a lot of work with the space of emotional wellness, no one should be in question that more is required. Emotional well-being can strike anyone, and it doesn't think about age, sexual orientation, culture, or calling. There are numerous reasons why emotional well-being can happen, and nobody's case can be viewed as something very similar.

In this chapter, we are proposing the utilization of emotional intelligence in supporting procedures to assist individuals with psychological well-being. Be that this blog entry is not a viable replacement for getting genuine clinical guidance and treatment as it may. Further, this blog ostensibly proposes something for individuals who may accept they are enduring at the lower ends of emotional wellness. The reason for this blog entry diagrams how the utilization of emotional intelligence could assist with the beginning of psychological wellness. In thought, emotional intelligence can be displayed with self-awareness, controlling feelings, inspiration, compassion, and relationship building.

Self-awareness is the capacity to survey own emotions and understanding the effect they can have on oneself. Through self-awareness, one can identify their own qualities and regions to improve. This by itself can give someone psychological wellness issues to see the value in their present position. Self-awareness is a center segment of emotional intelligence and has been tried in numerous fields. Inside psychological well-being, it is considered that at the lower levels, if one can get aware of their emotions, it might permit acknowledgment of issues significantly sooner. Psychological well-being is a significant theme, and reality would empower us to manage gives prior. As such, counteraction is superior to fix. Consequently, the execution of self-awareness gets vital for own psyche and equilibrium. For instance, if I am self-aware of my activities and can identify that these are not assisting me with controlling my emotions, I have begun to create awareness.

In light of this acknowledgment, I am ready to create systems to control my emotions. For instance, I may not make interpretations of more assignments as they increase stress, prompting poor emotional control. Moreover, I can also identify zones that I am performing admirably and utilize these to construct self-certainty. Certainly, through building self-certainty, one makes energy to improve attitude and sensation of happiness to work with balance.

The capacity to manage to feel could be essential for managing emotional wellness. Our emotions can vacillate for the duration of the day, and their very nature can direct whether we can handle these emotions. While encountering psychological well-being, it tends to be considered that minor issues become major because of failure to adapt. Managing feeling isn't simple and is something that should be drilled reliably. Regular methodologies to manage feeling incorporate defining objectives, care, profound breathing, contemplation, good self-talk, tuning in to music, and intelligent practice. Through defining objectives, one can recover center and bearing to finish undertakings.

Having accomplished these objectives, one can begin to recover emotional control. Care empowers us to remain right now. People tend to zero in on past and future occasions/potential outcomes. Critically we don't invest sufficient energy on the present. As such, the present is in our control, and we can take care of business. The past has gone, and what's to come isn't here. Consequently, it is recommended that individuals see their present circumstances and begin to set those little objectives that can be accomplished with the care. Care can assist individuals with liking their present circumstances and discover approaches to manage every viewpoint. For instance, profound breathing empowers individuals to remain in the present and gives more control to recover balance as a top priority and body. Contemplation is training that not all individuals will feel good with yet can be viable if utilized well. Reflection doesn't need to be strict based yet can also identify with different types of training.

Meditation can help emotional well-being victims by offering extension and center as one can rehearse profound breathing and substantial development to give energy. To be sure, an absence of energy is a typical factor related to emotional wellness. An increment in energy can also be significant as certain individuals with emotional wellness need energy and inspiration. Positive self-talk is a capacity to supplant negative contemplations however should be accepted and comes from the inside. Plainly, someone with emotional wellness may not feel good to change their reasoning.

Notwithstanding, some little changes can prompt energy, and one model could be from 'I can't do this to 'I will do this.' Music is an abstract technique yet one that has been demonstrated inside exploration to help lift state of mind and feeling. Adjusted to every one of these systems the utilization of intelligent practice is crucial. Intelligent practice will work with and support measures. Psychological wellness patients require support that they are progressing admirably, and intelligent practice gives them freedoms to self-survey their own advancement.

To empower development, inspiration is a need and need that has been proposed by scholars. We as a whole have inherent (inner) and extraneous (outer) needs. These requirements can be physical, physiological, mental, nourishment, and typically a blend of all. Inspiration can be all the more viably coordinated using measure objectives. Inside emotional wellness, one of the vital drivers to help individuals is the utilization of inspiration as it can make the necessary energy. Apparently, an absence of inspiration can be identified with one part of psychological well-being. Subsequently, the utilization of inspiration procedures could switch this pattern.

Sympathy is putting one from someone else's perspective. Individuals should rehearse the specialty of sympathy as it forestalls the segregation, and detachment that one can feel. Notwithstanding, there are openings with compassion that can be used. It is prescribed that sympathy empowers one to evaluate and analyze things from another's point of view.

Someone with emotional wellness can perceive compassion if they partner with an individual victim. To be sure, joining gatherings or meeting others can really be valuable to fabricate compassion.

The capacity to assemble connections can be the foundation of creating freedoms to help psychological wellness. Relationship building is a chance to meet new individuals and to perform on assignments that form attachment. Obviously, the idea of emotional wellness may deliver this difficulty however, inside existence, it very well may be conceivable. Building new and creating existing kinships can empower individuals to open up and additionally accomplish cognizance of trust. For sure, a foundation of emotional well-being is to open up and converse with individuals through relationship                                   building.

## 5.1motional Intelligence In The Workplace

The most sought-after characteristics in new position candidates have since quite a while ago included focuses like instruction, inspiration, experience, trustworthiness and certainty. All the more as of late, emotional intelligence has entered the program as perhaps the best qualities in people in the present labor force. Emotional intelligence, or EQ, assumes a crucial part in any worker's capacity to perform successfully as a component of an expert group.

Feeling and the individual association have for quite some time been a fairly untouchable theme in the working environment - this obsolete thought proposes that relational connection past the amazingly proficient is ineffective, best-case scenario, and hindering at more regrettable. Yet, this couldn't possibly be more off-base. Incidentally, emotionally keen representatives or gatherings with high EQ are more profitable and more fruitful than those without. Dynamic awareness and sympathy encourage group holding and aggregate inspiration: everybody is working for the accomplishment of the gathering, and the organization on the loose. It is to the greatest advantage of organizations wherever to welcome on workers with this exceedingly significant quality.

---

**The Value of Emotional Intelligence in the Workplace**

There are four particular classifications of emotional intelligence, which each offers one-of-a-kind advantages inside a workplace.

**Self-Awareness** permits us to understand ourselves. A worker with self-awareness has their very own expressive understanding qualities, shortcomings, drivers, values and their effect on others in the working environment. Their instinct is sharp, and they have a fair of how they fit into some random undertaking or job. They like accepting valuable analysis and are exceptionally energetic to improve their own exhibition and positively affect the remainder of the labor force.

**Self-Management** empowers us to feel negative emotions and keeps them from having a problematic effect. A worker with great self-administration abilities won't ever let dissatisfaction or anger hinder them from accomplishing their best work. Moreover, they will feel good drawing issues inside the working environment out into the open and support themself as well as other people in a fitting and expert tone. As a pioneer, they will empower, and control their group through disappointment while keeping up assurance, and solidarity.

**Social Awareness** is the thing that makes us extraordinary cooperative individuals. A worker with intense social awareness can tell when others are awkward, withdrawn, or aren't saying something they need to say. They put the prosperity of the gathering before their own prosperity and will account for bunch thought by working with a really collective climate. They are administration arranged, an incredible audience, and especially great openly confronting jobs.

**Relationship Management** is at its most essential applied sympathy. A worker with the relationship the executives abilities is naturally a specialist in compromise. They can try to avoid panicking, notwithstanding another's pain, and will actually want to diffuse the circumstance through humor or compassionate tuning in. They are profoundly persuasive in the working environment, and as a rule, make extraordinary candidates for the executive's positions.

Step by step instructions to Use Emotional Intelligence in the Workplace

### As a Leader

If you're a pioneer at your organization, you probably have a high EQ. That is on the grounds that pioneers should utilize emotional intelligence consistently busy working. Presidents, and individual group administrators the same should set the main social model for the remainder of the gathering, drawing in your workers the manner in which you need them to draw in with you, and one another. Moreover, you must be mindful to think about others' emotions - showing your representatives you regard them is simply the most ideal approach to acquire regard.

## Giving a Performance Review

Unfortunately, the criticism goes no place except if you give it with judgment and social awareness. Understanding what your representatives need and how they feel about themselves and their work can assist you with deciding the best method to transfer valuable analysis. Practicing sympathy and utilizing self-administration if your representative becomes disturbed can help persuade them to put forth a valiant effort and keep on succeeding.

## Getting Feedback

It very well may be difficult to get negative criticism. Particularly if you thought you were working effectively. Be that as it may, criticism is only a chance to improve, and while you may have an automatic response when another person discloses to us how we bombed them (we as a whole do now and then), with self-awareness, and self-administration we can respond suitably, and saddle input to better yourself, and become a more viable colleague.

## As a Hiring Manager

Testing a candidate for EQ abilities is the genuine test. Emotional intelligence can be instructed and trained; however, recruiting new representatives who are emotionally canny off the bat saves time, cash, and a ton of energy. Jen Shirkani suggests posing one inquiry during a meeting to evaluate EQ: "Have you at any point inadvertently insulted or vexed somebody? If it's not too much trouble, give subtleties." This inquiry tests the candidate's self-awareness, just as their capacity to address struggle and exercise sympathy. If they battle to discover an answer, they in all probability, have feeble EQ. If they give you a nitty-gritty story, confessing their slip-ups and disclosing how they dealt with rectify the circumstance, you may have discovered authority material.

---

## 5.2 Emotional Intelligence in The Relationships

Emotional intelligence can assist individuals with driving, and deal with their connections undeniably more successfully. Proof recommends that individuals with more elevated emotional intelligence levels lead more fruitful professions and support preferable connections over those with low emotional intelligence.

10 High-EQ Tips for Improving Family Relationships

1. **Deal with your health if you desire to deal with any other person**. The more demanding your family's time is, the more you need to fit in work out. Maybe you, and your family can search out approaches to practice together.

2. **Tune in if you hope to be heard.** The absence of correspondence is the most intense protest in many families. The response to "Is there any valid reason why they won't hear me out?" might be essential "You're not tuning in to them."

3. **Show emotional decision**. Deal with your states of mind by leaving all emotions alone OK, yet

not all practices. Model conduct that regards, and empowers the sentiments, and privileges of others yet clarify that we have a decision about how to manage what we feel.

4. **Show liberality by getting just as giving**. Giving and accepting are portions of a similar cherishing continuum. If we don't give, we think that it's difficult to get, and if we can't get it, we don't actually have a lot to give. This is the reason selflessness conveyed to limits is of little advantages to other people.

5. **Assume liability for what you impart quietly**. The exceptionally youthful, and old are particularly delicate to nonverbal prompts. More than our words, manner of speaking, pose (non-verbal communication) and outward appearances pass on our emotions. We need to tune in to our manner of speaking, and take a gander at ourselves in pictures, and in the mirror to evaluate our emotional congruency. Adoring words coming through gripped teeth don't feel cherishing—they feel confounding.

6. **Try not to attempt to take care of issues for your loved ones.** Really focusing on your family

doesn't mean assuming responsibility for their issues, offering spontaneous guidance, or shielding them from their own emotions. Tell them their own qualities and permit them to ask you for what they need.

7. **Establish a long-term connection through activities.** Your qualities will be imparted by your activities, regardless of what you say. Be a model, not a bother.

8. **Recognize your mistakes to everybody, including more youthful relatives.** Saying you're sorry when you hurt somebody you love models lowliness and emotional respectability. You can exhibit that nobody is awesome, yet everybody can learn at whatever stage in life. Saying 'sorry' demonstrates you can pardon yourself and makes it simpler to excuse others.

9. **Find what every individual's special necessities are.** You can't accept that your grandmother needs the very indications of love as your kid or that possibly one will have similar necessities one year from now. If all else fails, inquire!

10. **Be liberal in communicating love.** Everybody in a family (particularly small kids) needs the

emotional consolation of adoring words, signals and looks. The individuals who demand the most un-emotional consideration may require it most.

**The establishments of emotional intelligence in the family**

Look to yourself first. A family comprises related people, yet that doesn't mean you can reprimand your group of sources for the manner in which you are today; anything else than you can consider your mate and kids answerable for your own happiness. Your best expects fixing any family issue is to go to your own emotional wellbeing. At the point when you follow up on the conviction that you have a privilege and commitment to affirm your own emotional necessities, your family will see that your emotional autonomy benefits you, however, the entire family, and they may rapidly take cues from you.

**Recall that consistency constructs trust.** Studies have shown that the absence of consistency annihilates trust. Again, emotional awareness will cause the individuals who love and rely upon you, particularly kids, to get confounded and scared. That is the reason it's so critical to keep your awareness dynamic with family.

**Perceive that being close doesn't mean being clones.** At times family attaches daze us to the uniqueness of those we love. Pride in the family continuum can make it simple to fail to remember that. You can't be required to have similar abilities as your kin, despite the fact that you may look a ton the same; that you will not really decide to emulate parent's example; or that you, and your companion should invest all your recreation energy joined at the hip since you're hitched.

**Recall that knowing individuals for your entire life doesn't mean understanding them.** "I knew you when... " doesn't mean I know you presently, regardless of the amount I've generally loved you. As a whole, we change, yet every one of us appears to just see a change in ourselves. How enraging is it to be presented as somebody's child sibling when you're fifty-five, or to be ceaselessly treated as the numb skull you were at fourteen regardless of the way that you're currently CEO of your own organization. Since you've gained compassion, you can tenderly direct your family away from stale examples of communication by demonstrating the consideration you'd prefer to get. At the point when you're with your family, don't naturally look for the conversational shelter of talking over bygone eras. Ask what's going on, and show that you truly care by inspiring subtleties, and then tuning in with your body, and brain.

**Watch out for damaging emotional recollections.** Getting your thirty-year-old self reacting to a parent in the voice of the five-year-old you can cause you to feel feeble, and disappointed. With EQ, you don't have to continue to get trapped by emotional recollections. At whatever point you feel wild with family—regardless of whether it's kicking yourself for acting like a child with your folks or obsessing about where the anger you're unloading on your blameless life partner, and kids is coming from—pause for a minute to ponder the recollections that are forcing on your conduct today.

**Value each phase of life in every relative.** Regardless of how well we understand that it can't occur, we frantically need Mom, and Dad to remain the manner in which they are and for the children to remain at home for eternity. The best to acknowledge that reality emotionally is to accept change. Acknowledge the characteristic fear that your folks' maturing brings out, yet utilize your emotional awareness, and compassion to sort out how you can love this second for its one-of-a-kind characteristics. What can you, and your folks share now that was beyond the realm of imagination previously? Would you be able to continue to have a good time, and ensure everybody actually feels valuable, and commendable in the family emotionally supportive network, despite the fact that jobs, and duties should be adjusted?

If you don't know what will work, inquire. Completely tolerating your fear of progress can make it simpler to propose topics that you may have considered abnormal before. Possibly your folks are simply sitting tight for your prompt. Get a handle on them. In an adaptable, solid relational peculiarity, change is only one of the numerous changes you need to enhance each other.

Utilizing emotional intelligence to coexist with grown-up family members

Two components undermine agreeable relations with guardians, and grown-up kin, parents in law, and grown-up kids: absence of time, and a bounty of emotional recollections. The two amounts to the fear that we'll be overpowered by one another's requirements, surrendering ourselves if we offer anything to these grown-up family members. We do have to put the time in sorting out what our folks need most from us, supporting dear fellowships with siblings, and sisters and assembling without satisfying each terrible joke at any point expounded on disagreeable, selfish families.

However, emotional intelligence gives us such a lot of energy and imagination that these connections' demands don't should be substantial. We perceive change as it happens in people by perceiving emotional recollections when they're set off. Keep your EQ solid and your grown-up family experiences are not, at this point overwhelmed by tidying up after botches, and overseeing emergencies that have effectively brought about a catastrophe.

## Improving associations with your grown-up children

Numerous guardians are unnerved to find that they can't simply pause for a minute or two and appreciate their rewards for all the hard work once they've effectively guided their kids into adulthood. No relationship stands still. The way into a fruitful progressing relationship with your developed youngsters is your capacity to manage the change, and development that precedes job inversion. You need to keep the lines of emotional correspondence open; your kids might be enveloped with profession, love and companionships at this stage in their lives. Tell them how you feel, and what you need from them.

If you've as of late raised your EQ, obviously, you may make them correct to do, a few changes to make in your style of connection with your youngsters. Do they keep away from you since you power exhortation or your own decisions on them? Do you carry more disillusionment, and judgment to the relationship than they can endure? Have you listened empathically to how your youngsters feel about their decisions? Or then again have you attempted to discover what their novel requirements are? Some grown-up kids stay away on the grounds that they feel harmed by past encounters with you; all things considered, the best way to improve the connections is to adhere to these tips—tune in to their damage, and concede you weren't right. Here are a couple of approaches to overcome any barrier:

- Find out why it's so difficult to acknowledge your kids' decisions when they're different from your own. Utilize the hot catches investigation portrayed above, yet wonder why you feel so unequivocally about this issue, why you should be in charge and why you can't acknowledge their entitlement to settle on free decisions?

- Tap into the force of conciliatory sentiment. It's never past the point where it is possible to say, "I'm heartbroken, I wish I might have been a superior parent," "I wish I had done things any other way," or "You merited better compared to what I gave." Heartfelt expressions of sadness, and lament become especially incredible in a letter—as long as the letter is given as a gift without assumptions regarding what it will acquire in return. It might bring nothing with the exception of the information that you have put forth a valiant effort to directly past wrongs. You may also wish to inquire as to whether there is any way that you can offer peace.

- Explore what you anticipate from one another. If your alienated youngster is willing, every one of you should make a rundown of close to seven things regarding what you need and need from one another, what you think different needs, and needs from you. Presently think about records and perceive how close every one of you comes to addressing different necessities.

If your child is reluctant or you're reluctant to ask, you can, in any case, do this activity all alone. Round out the rundown for yourself, then move to another seat or position, and round out a rundown as you might suspect your grown-up kid would. Presently analyze. Is what your grown-up kid needs different based on the thing you're advertising? Have you neglected to perceive how the youngster has changed?

## Recovering your grown-up kin

In high-EQ families, siblings, and sisters split obligations regarding maturing guardians, and anticipate events to get every one of the ages together, on the grounds that they all know their cutoff points, and their gifts, and how to pass on them. Lamentably, this is certainly not an exact picture of numerous grown-up kin connections in light of the fact that again, and again, history intercedes. Possibly your folks didn't give the sort of love, and backing your sibling required just as they accomplished for you. Possibly beloved recollections trigger a lot of disdain, desire and competition. Possibly it just hurt a lot of the sister who realized you so well didn't mind enough to see how you've changed throughout the long term.

Whatever the issue, you can utilize any of the thoughts in this article to restore your relationship. If you have the opportunity, you can also take a stab at reconnecting by disappearing together, where you will both be agreeable, and undisturbed. Attempt an unstructured setting and utilize your time together to send a ton of "I feel" messages. Clarify that in communicating, you're not requesting that your kin change. At the point when your skin reacts, ensure you tune in with your body, not with counters arranged in your mind.

If your kin is difficult to reach and a trip will not work, can you reconnect by requesting help in a manner that recognizes their one-of-a-kind abilities? Consider ways you can cause your skin to feel remarkably required.

## Improving associations with your more distant family

How are your associations with your more distant family—those you're identified with by marriage or through looser direct relations? Stressed in light of the fact that you're attempting to frame family bonds without the emotional history to make them stick? Or then again, smooth since they don't accompany the emotional stuff that your close group of root hauls around? Either is conceivable in any individual relationship. How difficult one of these connections is may rely upon the fact that it is so imperative to you, and how long you've been busy. Coexisting with a brand-new relative, thusly mother has left disagreeable emotional recollections. Then again, it's presumably a snap to be sincere to the cousin you see just at occasion social affairs.

How great and profound your connections are with the more distant family generally rely on what you need them to be. We feel regretful if we hate our own folks, yet there's nothing that says we need to love our parents-in-law; such countless individuals don't feel committed to putting forth a tremendous attempt. Basically, stretch out a similar sympathy to your more distant family as you would to any other person you experience and that implies tolerating the wide scope of differences that will undoubtedly exist so you can track down the basic places of association.

Suppose you're also able to tune in with compassion regardless of who is talking, concede blunder and watch the nonverbal signals you send. In that case, you stand a very decent chance of turning into the universally adored niece, esteemed uncle, or model in-law. Expecting you haven't yet accomplished that state, here are a couple of tips to make more distant family connections fulfilling.

---

## 5.3 The Importance of Emotional Intelligence In Leadership

Business insight, logical abilities, experience and vision are, on the whole, attributes frequently connected with the best chefs, and authoritative pioneers. In any case, a disregarded quality found in the best supervisors is maybe the most basic: emotional intelligence.

Emotional intelligence (at times alluded to as EQ or EI) is the capacity to appreciate, control and build up your own sentiments while also having the option to understand, and deal with others' sentiments. Emotional intelligence goes past the authoritative stray pieces of being an extraordinary pioneer, and underlines what your emotions mean for other people, and how you can utilize that information to make positive results — both actually, and with individuals you oversee.

Raj Sisodia, in his part of Servant Leadership in real life: How You Can Achieve Great Relationships, and Results, says, "Emotional intelligence (EQ) consolidates self-awareness (understanding oneself), and sympathy (the capacity to feel, and understand what others are feeling). High emotional intelligence is progressively being perceived as significant in associations in light of the developing intricacy of society, and the assortment of partners that should be spoken with viably."

The emotional intelligence approach is something of an extreme takeoff from the conventional administration style of "I say 'bounce,' you say 'how high?'" Leadership actually requires an authority over the group's vision, yet it should be interlaced with putting workers, and their necessities first. This affirmation from the administration makes more joyful, more gainful specialists, and more successful administrators, while also lessening representative turnover.

## Advantages for the Leader

Pioneers who show, and sustain high emotional intelligence unavoidably become better pioneers. Think about these advantages:

- **Internal awareness:** Making steady choices requires understanding what your sentiments are meaning for judgment, profitability, perspectives, and more. The best chiefs are self-aware of their emotions and their shortcomings and constraints, just as their qualities. For instance, a supervisor who is anything, but a decent delegator however is self-aware about that weakness can put forth a cognizant attempt to designate out errands more, and trust individuals those undertakings have been appointed to. Inside awareness isn't disposing of emotions from choices, yet rather permitting them to work with discernment so they don't subliminally influence judgment.

- **Self-guideline:** Leaders who settle on indiscreet choices or neglect to control their emotions and lash out can rapidly lose their subordinates' admiration. Those unregulated minutes can fix any compatibility you've constructed —, and getting it back is rarely simple. Emotional intelligence breeds self-guideline that forestalls the minutes you wish you could reclaim.

- **Expanded empathy**: People with high emotional intelligence have their very own decent understanding of emotional states, which permits them to precisely measure others' emotions. This sympathy places them from their workers' point of view for business pioneers, hence prompting more insightful, and conscious choices.

- **Collaborative communication:** Because they understand their associates, emotionally keen pioneers can quickly get the tone of the room or bunch, and along these lines talk with trustworthiness, and truthfulness to coordinate with that tone or alleviate uncertain strain.

- **Less pressure**: Workplace stress might be unavoidable, yet pioneers with emotional intelligence oversee it better, and don't allow it to devour them. They also decline to take any negative emotions out on their associates or families. In general, these pioneers appreciate better work/life balance, realizing that the emotions of work need to remain at work (and the other way around).

## Advantages for the Organization

A lot of associations with an apparently interminable inventory of specialized skill, and long periods of involvement keep on battling in light of the fact that they need emotional intelligence. These organizations also experience difficulty forestalling worker turnover. On the other hand, organizations with high emotional intelligence appreciate numerous benefits, including:

- **Better team involvement:** Teams that vibe a negative connection — or no connection by any means — to group pioneers or their colleagues withdraw, and, accordingly, neglect to profit by the inborn advantages of filling in collectively. Emotional intelligence recognizes the group dynamic and gives everybody a voice.
- **Improved organization culture:** Organizations regularly talk about how incredible their organizational culture is, yet without emotional intelligence, what you think your way of life is may differ from what your workers really feel. Edgar H.

Schein, and Peter A. Schein write in Humble Leadership: The Power of Relationships, Openness and Trust, "In our view, authority is consistently a relationship,, and really fruitful initiative flourishes in a gathering society of high receptiveness, and high trust." Leaders with emotional intelligence empower more grounded connections, and open correspondence, which draws you nearer to the way of life the organization probably needs to accomplish.

- **High execution drove outcomes:** Trusted workers, whose emotions are esteemed and who haven't oppressed the negative, unfiltered emotions of their bosses, just perform better —, and greater efficiency, at last, improves the main concern.

These advantages are share something common: The improved emotional intelligence pioneers have created positive outcomes in their workers. As Robert Johansen writes in The New Leadership Literacies: Thriving in a Future of Extreme Disruption, and Distributed Everything, "If pioneers flourish in an eventual fate of outrageous disturbance, they should not just deal with their own energy, they should empower, model and positive prize energy in others."

## Chapter 6. Myths About Emotional Intelligence

The abilities of emotional intelligence are amazing, without a doubt. The capacity to identify different emotions, understand their impact, and utilize that data to manage thinking and conduct significantly builds the odds of effectively accomplishing your objectives. A high EQ can make you a more successful pioneer and can improve the nature of your own connections.

Be that as it may, there's a ton to misunderstand about emotional intelligence.

Here's we investigate some of these legends and shows exactly how EQ functions and doesn't function in reality.

For instance, here are seven of the main fantasies about EQ:

### 1. Emotional Intelligence Doesn't Exist.

Truly, emotional intelligence as a scientific examination field is generally new and even specialists differ on its application.

Although the terms emotional intelligence, EI and EQ are just many years old, the ideas aren't. Antiquated religions and savants have advanced thoughts like the accompanying for quite a long time:

- "Everyone should rush to tune in, moderate to talk, moderate to anger."
- "Care for your mind... know thyself, for once we know ourselves, we may figure out how to really focus on ourselves."
- "To see is to endure."

As emotional animals, we should recognize the job our sentiments play in impacting thinking and dynamics. Really at that time, would we be able to start attempting to understand them.

## 2. Emotional Intelligence Is Just Common Sense.

Some contend that emotional intelligence is basically an extravagant term for what the greater part of us knows better as "sound judgment," characterized by Merriam-Webster as "the capacity to think, and act sensibly, and to use sound judgment."

In any case, that detracts from the truth of EI: It requires incredible exertion and profound thought to understand emotional conduct, both our own and others –, and the explanations for it. Also, even the least difficult EI abilities, for example, stopping to think before we talk, are a lot simpler in principle than they are practically speaking.

### 3. You Can Control Your Feelings.

Hopefully, we will self-manage our emotions, dialing back on our anger when we feel ourselves letting completely go (for instance).

In any case, emotions include our regular, natural sentiments. Now, and again, these are because of a specific circumstance or occasion; on different occasions, they're impacted by our own mind science. As such, we can't generally control how we feel.

What we can handle is our response to those sentiments. By getting aware of what our emotions mean for us and then zeroing in on our contemplations, we can regularly keep our emotions from making us act unreasonably.

### 4. Emotional People are More Emotionally Intelligent.

If you're the sort that cries effectively when watching a sad film, that could be an indication that you have compassion and can undoubtedly identify with others' sentiments.

Be that as it may, an excess of sympathy can undoubtedly be utilized against you. Imagine a scenario in which a "companion" is continually introducing a tragic account to get you to cover for them while they proceed in some self-damaging conduct. Compassion may move you to help them consistently, even though it's not actually what you need to do—and is also not what's best for your companion.

The capacity to "feel" others' emotions is an important apparatus, yet it's just a single ability. You're a one-of-a-kind individual with a novel emotional reaction system. Creating emotional intelligence requires understanding how your emotions work and then adequately dealing with those emotions to accomplish your own objectives.

## 5. Sharpening Your EQ Is Easy.

Despite what might be expected, creating emotional intelligence is quite possibly the most difficult difficulties you'll at any point face.

Consider everything: We're brought into the world with emotions, so our emotional conduct is a long time really taking shape. Also, researchers have shown that endeavoring to roll out enduring improvements to conduct is a compound cycle that requires considerable responsibility.

If you're not kidding about expanding your EQ, you must be in it for the long stretch.

**6. Whenever You've Got It, You've Got It.**

Since a horde of elements impacts your (and others) emotions, it's not difficult to fall once again into detrimental routines or endure an episode of awful dynamic.

Further, with regards to understanding others' sentiments and emotions, time neutralizes us. Examination demonstrates that regardless of whether we've encountered a similar circumstance as to another, we don't recall it just as we might suspect we do.

That makes dealing with your emotional intelligence a persistent interaction.

**7. Those With High Emotional Intelligence Always Make The Best Leaders.**

Regardless of EI's capability for great, there's an equivalent limit with respect to it to be utilized to adventure, menace, and abuse others. Therapists have recorded how narcissists and egomaniacs utilize emotionally canny abilities to control others.

Obviously, that is only one more justification for you to hone your own emotional intelligence–to ensure yourself when they do.

## Chapter 7. How To Develop Your EQ

With regards to happiness, and accomplishment in life, EQ matters similarly as much as IQ. Figure out how you can support your emotional intelligence, fabricate more grounded connections and accomplish your objectives.

### For what reason is emotional intelligence so significant?

As far as we might be concerned, the sharpest individuals aren't the best or the most satisfied in life. You most likely know scholastically splendid individuals and yet are socially maladroit and fruitless at work or in their own connections. Scholarly capacity or your intelligence quotient (IQ) isn't sufficient all alone to make progress in life. In fact, your IQ can help you with getting to school. However, it's your EQ that will assist you with dealing with the pressure and emotions when confronting your last tests of the year. Intelligence level and EQ exist in tandem and are best when they work off each other.

### Four key skills to expanding your EQ

The skills that make up emotional intelligence can be learned at any time. However, there is a difference between simply learning about EQ and applying that knowledge to your life. Stress, for example, can override your best intentions and even you know you should do something in that circumstance doesn't mean you will. To permanently change behavior, you need to learn how to overcome stress in the moment and in your relationships to remain emotionally aware.

The critical abilities for building your EQ and improving your capacity to oversee emotions and interface with others are:

1. Self-management

2. Self-awareness

3. Social awareness

4. Relationship management

**Self-Management**

With the goal for you to draw in your EQ, you should be capable utilize your emotions to settle on useful choices about your conduct. When you become excessively focused, you can fail to keep a grip on your emotions and the capacity to act nicely and properly.

Consider when stress has overpowered you. Was it simple to think unmistakably or settle on a sane choice?

Most likely not. When you become excessively focused, your capacity to both think plainly and precisely survey emotions—your own and other people's—gets traded off.

Emotions are significant snippets of data that enlighten you concerning yourself as well as other people, and however, despite the stress that removes us from our usual range of familiarity, we can get overpowered and fail to keep a grip on ourselves. With the capacity to oversee pressure and stay emotionally present, you can figure out how to get disturbing data without allowing it to abrogate your musings and self-control. You'll have the option to settle on options that permit you to control incautious sentiments,and practices, deal with your emotions healthy, step up to the plate, finish responsibilities and adjust to evolving conditions.

**Self-Awareness**

Overseeing pressure is only the initial step to building emotional intelligence. The study of connection shows that your present emotional experience is likely an impression of your initial life experience. Your capacity to oversee center sentiments like anger, sadness, fear and bliss regularly relies upon the quality, and consistency of your initial life emotional encounters. If your primary overseer as a newborn child comprehended and esteemed your emotions, your emotions may have become significant resources in grown-up life. Yet, if your emotional encounters as a newborn child were befuddling, undermining or agonizing, it's probably you've attempted to remove yourself from your emotions.

Be that as it may, having the option to associate with your emotions—having a second-to-second association with your changing emotional experience—is the way to understanding what feeling means for your musings and activities.

**Do you encounter sentiments that stream,** experiencing one feeling after another as your encounters change from one second to another?

**Are your emotions joined by actual impressions that you experience** in places like your stomach, throat, or chest?

**Do you encounter singular sentiments and emotions,** like anger, sadness, fear and bliss, every one of which is clear in unpretentious outward appearances?

**Would you be able to encounter extreme emotions** that are sufficiently able to catch both your consideration, and that of others?

**Do you focus on your emotions?** Do they factor into your dynamic?

If any of these encounters are new, you may have "turned down" or "killed" your emotions. To fabricate EQ—and become emotionally sound—you should reconnect to your center emotions, acknowledge them and become alright with them. You can accomplish this through the act of care.

**Mindfulness** is the act of intentionally concentrating on the current second—and without judgment. The development of care has been established in Buddhism. However, most religions incorporate some sort of comparative supplication or contemplation strategy. Care helps shift your distraction with thought toward enthusiasm for the occasion, your physical and emotional sensations and welcomes a bigger viewpoint on life. Care quiets and centers you, making you more self-aware all the while.

**Social awareness**

Social awareness empowers you to perceive and decipher the principally nonverbal signs others are continually utilizing to speak with you. These signs let you know how others are truly feeling, how their emotional state is changing from one second to another and what's really critical to them.

When gatherings of individuals convey comparative nonverbal signs, you're ready to peruse and understand the force elements and shared emotional encounters of the gathering. To put it plainly, you're sympathetic and socially agreeable.

## Mindfulness is a partner of emotional and social awareness

To fabricate social awareness, you need to perceive the significance of care in the social interaction. You can't get on inconspicuous nonverbal prompts when you're in your own head, contemplating different things, or just daydreaming on your telephone. Social awareness requires your essence at the time. While large numbers of us pride ourselves on a capacity to perform multiple tasks, this implies that you'll miss the unobtrusive emotional shifts occurring in others that assist you with understanding them.

- You are in reality bound to additional your social objectives by saving different contemplations and zeroing in on the communication itself.
- Following the progression of someone else's emotional reactions is a give-and-take measure that expects you to also focus on the adjustments in your own emotional experience.
- Paying thoughtfulness regarding others doesn't reduce your own self-awareness. By contributing the time and exertion to truly focus on others, you'll really acquire knowledge into your own emotional state just as your qualities and convictions. For instance, if you feel distress hearing others express certain perspectives, you'll have picked up something significant about yourself.

**Relationship management**

Cooperating with other people is an interaction that starts with emotional awareness and your capacity to perceive and understand what others are encountering. When emotional awareness is in play, you can adequately build up extra friendly/emotional abilities that will make your connections more powerful, productive and satisfying.

**Become aware of how adequately you utilize nonverbal correspondence.** It's difficult to try not to send nonverbal messages to others about your opinion and feel. The numerous muscles in the face, particularly those around the eyes, nose, mouth, and temple, help you silently pass on your own emotions just as perused other people groups' emotional plan. The emotional piece of your mind is consistently on—and regardless of whether you disregard its messages—others will not. Perceiving the nonverbal messages that you ship off others can have an enormous impact in improving your connections.

**Use humor and play to soothe pressure.** Humor, giggling, and play are regular cures to pressure. They decrease your weights, and help you keep things in context. Chuckling brings your sensory system into balance, diminishing pressure, quieting you down, honing your psyche, and making you more empathic.

**Figure out how to consider struggle to be a chance to develop nearer to other people.** Struggle and conflicts are unavoidable in human connections. Two individuals can't in any way, shape or form have similar requirements, sentiments and assumptions consistently. Notwithstanding that needn't be something terrible.

Settling struggle in solid, helpful ways can strengthen trust between individuals. When struggle isn't seen as compromising or rebuffing, it cultivates opportunity, imagination and wellbeing seeing someone.

## Building up Your Emotional Intelligence

**Deal with your negative emotions**. At the point when you're ready to oversee and diminish your negative emotions, you're less inclined to get overpowered. Actually quite difficult, isn't that so? Attempt this: If somebody is disturbing you, don't make quick judgment calls. All things being equal, permit yourself to take a gander at the circumstance in an assortment of ways. Attempt to take a gander at things equitably so you don't get bothered up as without any problem. Practice care at work and notice how your point of view changes.

**Practice compassion**. Focusing on verbal and non-verbal signals can give you significant understanding of your associates or customers' sensations. Work on zeroing in on others, and strolling from their perspective, regardless of whether only briefly. Compassionate explanations don't pardon unsuitable conduct, yet they help advise you that everybody has their own issues.

**Know your stressors.** Assess what worries you and be proactive to have less of it in your life. If you realize that browsing your work email before bed will send you into a spiral, leave it for the first part of the day. Even better, leave it for when you show up to the workplace.

**Use a self-assured way of conveying.**

Confident correspondence goes far toward procuring regard without appearing to be excessively forceful or excessively uninvolved. Emotionally astute individuals realize how to impart their suppositions and requirements in an immediate manner while as yet regarding others.

**Respond instead of reacting to conflict.**

During occurrences of contention, emotional upheavals and sensations of anger are normal. The emotionally astute individual realizes how to remain quiet during distressing circumstances. They don't settle on hasty choices that can prompt significantly more serious issues. They understand that in the midst of contention, the objective is a goal and they settle on a cognizant decision to zero in on guaranteeing that their activities and words are in arrangement with that.

## Use undivided attention abilities.

In discussions, emotionally canny individuals tune in for lucidity rather than simply trusting that their turn will talk. They ensure they understand what is being said prior to reacting. They also focus on the nonverbal subtleties of a discussion. This forestalls misunderstandings, permits the audience to react appropriately, and shows regard for the individual they are addressing.

## Practice ways to maintain a positive attitude.

Try not to belittle the force of your disposition. An adverse mentality effectively taints others if an individual permit it to. Emotionally clever individuals have an awareness of the temperaments of everyone around them and gatekeeper their demeanor likewise. They understand what they need to do to have a decent day and an idealistic standpoint. This could incorporate having an extraordinary breakfast or lunch, taking part in petition or reflection during the day or keeping positive statements at their work area or PC.

## Be approachable and sociable.

Emotionally keen individuals appear to be agreeable. They grin and radiate a positive presence. They use proper social abilities dependent on their relationship with whomever they are near. They have incredible relational abilities and skill to impart unmistakably, regardless of whether the correspondence is verbal or nonverbal.

**Bob back from difficulty.** Everybody experiences difficulties. It's the means by which you respond to these difficulties that either sets you up for progress or puts you on the track to full on emergency mode. You definitely realize that positive reasoning will benefit you. To help you ricochet back from affliction, practice good faith as opposed to grumbling. What would you be able to gain from the present circumstance? Pose valuable inquiries to perceive what you can detract from the test at hand.

Emotional intelligence can develop over the long haul as long as you want to expand it. Each individual, challenge, or circumstance confronted is an excellent learning freedom to test your EQ. It takes practice, however, you can begin receiving the rewards right away.

## Chapter 8. Obstacles to the improvement of EQ

A group of clinicians drove by Dr. Jean-Charles Lebeau out of Florida State University as of late directed an examination taking a gander at the impact of disappointment on execution. The scientists found that encountering difficulties contrarily impacts your emotions and self-viability however has no impact on genuine execution results. Conquering obstructions, it ends up, is a significant piece of the interaction.

The discoveries challenge the prevailing perspective that disappointment is awful on the grounds that it harms an individual's ability to be self aware viability, which thus prompts more disappointment. As indicated by the examination, while disappointment does for sure damage self-viability, the mental succession stops there. A disappointment at Time 1 doesn't really mean more disappointment at Time 2.

Truth be told, disappointment in such cases can really help drive achievement. The new exploration recommends that the appropriate response lies by the way you adapt to your emotional reaction to snags.

## Transforming disappointment into fuel for conquering hindrances

Bombing sucks. You've certainly encountered the disaster of not arriving at an objective and the emotional droop that goes with it. The terrible news is that the awful inclination you get after you come up short is practically unavoidable. In any case, fortunately, even though you're probably going to feel less equipped for accomplishing an objective after you fall flat, you will not really perform more terribly the following time around. Indeed, it very well may be disappointment itself that impels you forward towards accomplishing your objective, paying little heed to how awful you feel.

The thought that disappointment drives achievement is officially known as the control hypothesis. Defenders of the control hypothesis see disappointment and execution as a cycle much the same as that of an indoor regulator: with the rising warmth of disappointment, your mind's interior lead representative kicks in to chill your presentation off the street.

Control hypothesis proposes that it is imperative to encounter negative emotions when you come up short to succeed a while later. However, there's a kicker – it's no, and a wide range of emotions that work. Fundamentally, you track down the sweet spot between incapacitating negative emotions and the sort that fuel your control system.

The accompanying advances will help you track down that sweet spot in defeating snags.

**Stage 1: Recognize, and concede disappointment**

The initial step is conceding that you wrecked. This can be hard. Truth be told, we are mentally wired to do the specific inverse. Defeating deterrents expect you to confront the approaching presence of cacophony you experience when your endeavors are tested. In any case, as per control hypothesis, all together for our inside indoor regulator to kick in and make a move against disappointment, it initially requires the commencement of negative (emotional) criticism.

Here are two inquiries to pose to yourself when telling the truth about your disappointment:

- What caused the disappointment? In a request to change your disappointment into fuel for your own interests, it's fundamental that the reason for the disappointment is in your control. At the point when you ask yourself what caused your disappointment, you are giving yourself a decision. You can either assume full liability or re-appropriate the fault to a situational factor (a mistake in self/other judgment, which analysts call the essential attribution blunder).

- Could it have been kept away from? This is the place where the control hypothesis indoor regulator begins to work. While conceding your disappointment, it's significant that you are sure that it might have been kept away from if you had acted as per your objectives. Thusly, you are boosting your interior drive to fix the issue, pushing ahead. You're planning for activity.

## Stage 2: Turn off the reasoning

When the disappointment is conceded, the following stage in conquering snags is to plan and set expectations. You hear a great deal about looking on the brilliant side of disappointment. Despite the fact that gaining from it is fundamental for pushing forward, your quick emotional reaction doesn't need to be positive. Research discloses to us it shouldn't.

Studies propose that participating in emotional legitimization may really forestall your improvement in ensuing assignments. Moreover, endeavoring to change your negative sentiments into good ones really improves the probability of those negative emotions reemerging in a maladaptive manner over the long haul.

You need to insure yourself against this. Here are two basic reappraisal/concealment procedures to stay away from when confronting disappointment. Ask yourself, truly, regardless of whether you believe you're taking part in any of the accompanying:

- **Shoulda, coulda, woulda style thinking:** When you concoct a rationalization for why you should have, might have or would have done X if Y hadn't happened, you are basically stripping yourself of the ability to change your own condition. As indicated by control hypothesis, the solitary negative input that works in your inward system is your own activity, which implies it's fundamental to try not to think back on how outside factors subverted your prosperity.

- **Self-handicapping**: This is the point at which you put your disappointment on the way that you didn't anticipate prevailing in the first place. Thusly, you are fundamentally disclosing to yourself that you simply aren't ready to deal with the work. This perspective is futile since it doesn't give your inward components any input to work with. Your indoor regulator is broken.

### Stage 3: Turn on the inclination

So if you're not taking part in these post-hoc justifications, what's happening with you? You need to escape your head, and into your feels. We're regularly advised to abrogate our emotional reactions to disappointment with even tempered sanity. However, what exploration shows us is it's significant you display self-empathy by permitting yourself to encounter the hurt that accompanies disappointment.

Here are two different ways you can explore your negative emotions when managing disappointment:

- Pinpoint your careful emotional reaction: When exploring your emotional reaction to disappointment, it's imperative to specifically identify the sentiments and emotions that are evoked by your experience. Examination in clinical science discloses to us that the capacity to mark your negative emotions makes it more obvious how they're doing you.

- Identify what the inclination is asking you to do: Emotions frequently push us towards activity (or inaction). When you are confronted with a negative full of feeling state subsequent to encountering disappointment, set aside the effort to survey what the feeling is asking you to do. This prompts the main last advance all the while: making a movie.

## Stage 4: Assess your status for activity

You've conceded to your disappointment, fended off the desire to gloss over the circumstance and have set aside the effort to survey your emotional reaction. Presently it's an ideal opportunity to lock in and act.

As indicated by Dr. Nico Frijda, emotions (especially negative ones) are apparatuses to set you up for the activity. In any case, certain emotions are more powerful for starting the activity. You need to wind up encountering the kinds of "negative" emotions that will bump you toward activity (as opposed to inaction).

The circumplex model of emotions depicts emotional states as existing in a crossing circumplex of two measurements. One measurement portrays the valence of the feeling (for example, negative or positive) while the other measurement portrays the condition of excitement (for example, high or low). For instance, anger would fall on the upper left of the circumplex making it a high-excitement negative emotional state.

## Chapter 9. Proven strategies to improve your social awareness, and relationship management

Social awareness is the capacity to understand and react to circumstances in a superior manner. It implies how to respond to social circumstances. Additionally, it is the capacity to react successfully. Moreover, social awareness assists you with building solid connections. Be it individual connections or expert. Social awareness is exceptionally connected to emotional intelligence. It is one of the kinds of emotional intelligence. When you work on building up your social awareness abilities, you will be more esteemed. For example, a few instances of social awareness are the server proposing better decisions from the menu. Or then again, the sales rep is going the additional mile. These are a few occurrences of social awareness abilities that advantage connections.

### 7 ways to improve your social awareness

These social abilities exercises can assist you with improving your social awareness.

### 1. Give importance to listening

We generally believe that we are acceptable audience members. Be that as it may, as a general rule, we are quickly drawn off track by the smallest of interruption. Moreover, we continue to consider what should be our reaction to what in particular is being said. Be that as it may, this isn't the means by which a decent audience acts. Great audience members never judge the circumstance they know the truth. They don't go about as though they know about the circumstance. They center around tuning in and breaking down. They center around the thing is being said, and then search for emotions to improve your social awareness.

Moreover, when you are quiet with individuals, you will be surprised to know numerous things. A decent audience is constantly valued for his abilities. Also, they are esteemed in any association.

## 2. Make it a practice to repeat what is said

Is it accurate to say that you were tuning in? This is the ideal opportunity to demonstrate it. If you have been effectively tuning in, odds are you will actually want to rehash them. Also, when you rehash what is said, you can acquire data. Furthermore, if you missed something, the speaker can address it out for you. At the point when you rehash, you show your mindfulness.

Likewise, this also exhibits this; his/her words are heard, and values. Undivided attention prompts better trust and understanding of individuals. This is exceptionally advantageous in an association.

## 3. Focus on the tone

How something is said can have altogether different implications if said in different tones. Also, it is essential to know the energy of the tone. It is essential to understand what is being said. For example, something said decidedly could be misconstrued. Henceforth, focus on the tone of the speaker. Moreover, a person's tone can help you read how they feel about something. It also permits you to settle on a superior reaction and it assists with improving your social awareness.

## 4. Watch out for the non-verbal communication

This one is a significant ability that should be dominated. Actually, it is also perhaps the most disregarded sorts of abilities. Furthermore, an individual's non-verbal communication and articulations can reveal to you how they feel. This sort of ability will clearly set aside effort to dominate, however they are certainly feasible. Watch out for non-verbal communication and articulations to acquire data.

## 5. Place yourself in other's shoes

Sympathy and empathy assist you with understanding different points of view. Being merciful is imperative for sound connections. Also, it helps correspondence and critical thinking as well. Additionally, it expands your viewpoints and view circumstances in a different light.

For example, you are standing in a line at a supermarket. The clerk is setting aside a great deal of effort to handle each request. You begin becoming annoyed. Stop in that general area and think from the clerk's side. He may be a renewed individual attempting to gain proficiency with his work.

For what reason should he rush while learning? Venturing into other's perspectives will make you more quiet and understanding. Additionally, it gives you an understanding into their issues and improves your social awareness.

## 6. Identify your own emotions

It very well may be difficult to understand others if we can't mark and understand our emotions. The ideal approach to identify your emotions is to converse with somebody. Sharing your emotions will assist you with getting input. Furthermore, you can acquire a different point of view on your emotions. You can also work on composing a dairy. Record what you feel like, and name each feeling.

## 7. Reflect back

It is also critical to tell the individual how you feel when they share something. This assists you with understanding an individual. Additionally, your input also fulfills the other individual. It is important to show your appreciation for other people. Also, it is a significant factor in creating social awareness.

If you are hoping to create incredible connections and assemble real fellowships, you need to chip away at these abilities. Moreover, it structures incredible cooperations that help assemble social awareness. Essentially, take responsibility for conduct, and request criticism. It is also critical to see the practices of others that may make you react adversely.

## The Strategies To Improve Your Relationship Management

Regardless of whether you run an enormous organization with many representatives or a private company that knows its clients' entirety by name, extraordinary relationship the board abilities will consistently separate you from your rivals and assist you with holding clients.

Here you'll acquire 10 relationship executive abilities – from the force of going past the ordinary degree of client assistance to reviewing your clients and learning their requirements – that will improve your client maintenance rate. Are you new to the universe of business? Regardless of whether you're beginning a private company or expanding from an independent activity into an assistance centered organization, try out our Customer Service Training course to get familiar with the rudiments of aiding your clients.

## Awareness of client needs

Unless you understand what your clients need, you'll battle to stand out for them and persuade them to work with you. Realizing your industry's needs is a fundamental piece of showing your worth to possibilities and building connections.

Perhaps the most ideal approaches to becoming familiar with your objective market are reviewing existing clients to find out about what they do and don't esteem. You can do this utilizing on the web reviews and meeting structures that simplify assemble data.

## Direct promoting abilities

Many organizations cautiously screen the measure of cash they spend on client securing, yet not their time. Your time is important and having the option to quantify your time estimation makes figuring your relationship the board ROI basic.

Become familiar with the essentials of direct showcasing – from the expense of your chance to improving your business change rate –, and you'll see it simpler to shape business associations with new clients and keep up joins with your current client base.

## The capacity to associate with strangers

Reaching out to possibilities and transforming them into clients isn't simple. Indeed, even the most skilled sales reps feel nervous and fear when a specific possibility is less interested in working together than they recently envisioned.

Quite possibly, the main relationship the board abilities is the capacity to coexist with strangers. From cold pitches to prospects met at career expos and occasions, transformation and influence make relationship the executives far simpler.

**Aspiration and inspiration**

A goal-oriented, inspired mentality is fundamental for business achievement. Individuals that will contact prospects and call existing clients to realize what they're keen on quite often dominate past their careless, inactive partners.

There's nothing amiss with being yearning in deals and client assistance – truth be told, in the period of robotized client care and online help structures, a lot of your clients will see the value in addressing an agent that often thinks about them.

**Deals pipe information**

Site Marketing Concept BlackboardIt's significantly harder to get your first clients than it is to get your second. Numerous private companies battle with relationships the board since they can't obtain new clients at the correct expense, and speed for steady development.

Quite possibly the main relationship the executive abilities is the capacity to get new clients while holding existing ones. The most simple approach to do this is with a computerized, systematized deals channel.

**Vital reasoning abilities**

When you're overseeing under 100 clients, it's feasible to get by with no technique. Nonetheless, when you're overseeing associations with a huge number of clients, the capacity to shape techniques gets fundamental for progress.

Despite how great your client assistance abilities are, it's difficult to oversee connections utilizing a group without a technique set up. From guides for taking care of the most well-known issues to straightforward standards, relationship methodologies matter.

## Higher perspective reasoning

Customer administration and relationship the executives isn't just about keeping clients keen on working with you – it's tied in with framing connections that permit your business to advance close by its clients.

Along these lines, it's fundamental to know about the master plan – the manner in which your business finds a way into the lives and needs of your clients. What advantages do you offer, and for what reason do clients work with you rather than a contender?

## A well-disposed, individual disposition

When you work with another organization, you're not managing a solid corporate element, yet with individuals that it's made out of. Having the option to remain both expert and cordial is one of the critical highlights of fruitful administrators.

Effort to find some kind of harmony between the significance of demonstrable skill and the advantages of being amicable and friendly with key clients and customers. In numerous businesses – especially IT – a less conventional mentality is regularly an advantage in framing connections.

## Fabulous exploration abilities

From discovering somebody's email address to finding columnists that are keen on composing your item, having the option to explore your intended interest group and figure out how to get in touch with them is fundamental for framing business connections.

Probably the ideal approaches to investigate individuals is through imaginative re-appropriating. With a VA (menial helper) in your group, it's feasible to uncover new possibilities and figure out how to reach them while you center around your day-by-day plan for the day.

## Build up your relationship the board abilities today

The capacity to frame new connections and oversee old ones is which isolates extraordinary administrators from normal ones. At the point when you can connect with individuals, clarify what your business has to bring to the table, and close arrangements, you'll rapidly dominate in front of your companions.

- Understand client psychology

- The quintessence of client assistance brain research identifies with consumer loyalty. At the point when you understand your client needs altogether is the point at which you can support consumer loyalty rates. Clients hope to be esteemed, tuned in, though often about their concern, and need confirmation that the equivalent will not be rehashed later on.

- Client brain research can be investigated and perceived depending on their conduct and emotions to help you serve them better. The fundamental advantages your brand can acquire by understanding the brain research of clients are:

- Customer dependability – when clients are happy with your administration, they become your steadfast clients and be related with your brand.

- Brand support – when you know your client's inclinations, interests you can customize your discussions and fabricate a solid client relationship. Afterward, share their examples of overcoming adversity and promoter your brand.

- At the point when a client contacts you with a protest or issue, their assumption is to be heard and sort the issue out quickly. They expect a mindful ear who recognizes their concern and convey the correct arrangement.

**Focus on client experience**

Client experience is a basic piece of techniques to keep up client connections. Brands with predominant client experience get 5.7 occasions more income than contenders that slack in client experience.

The three significant advantages of building client connections that any business can observe are client reliability, maintenance and references. They straightforwardly affect the income of your business. When clients become steadfast, their lifetime esteem increments, and there are odds of prescribing you to likely new clients.

Glad and fulfilled clients stay steadfast. Understand the client excursion, and attempt to convey predictable client experience across the entire lifecycle. The more joyful are your clients, they will hold your business.

Make an incentive for clients

How would you snare a client for a lifetime?

As a brand, you need to zero in on making an incentive for your clients., and you can do as such by

- **Understanding your client needs** – Listen to what your clients say, their activities, and responses to understand what is significant for them, and search for the chances you can help them.
- **Build people group** – Communities can substantially affect key business execution markers. Organizations acquire a significant ascent in operational proficiency, income age and consumer loyalty. Subsequently, client networks can be identified as one of the primary methods to fabricate client connections.
- **Understand your incentive** – You need to understand what esteem your items or administrations makes for your clients. What will be the expense for them regarding utilization?
- **Invest in your important clients** – Allocate your business development towards new items, and arrangements that serve your best clients. Clients are the lifeblood of your business. They are the wellspring of current benefits, and the establishment of future development.

- **Educate clients** – Businesses receive different showcasing ploys to bait possibilities. Clients are bound to confide in those brands that put forth an attempt to improve their insight about their items or administrations. Exploration expresses that teaching clients strengthens their trust in an association and it can go about as a significant help differentiator for brands.

---

## Conclusion

The activities we make in our lives are generally founded on our emotions and emotional intelligence. It makes sense that when people have an extraordinary feeling of correspondence and hierarchical abilities, they will be lead to being able to settle on legitimate choices and connections with others. What we gain from our own emotions will permit us to seek after the lifestyle we need to live and make a greater amount of what we need in our lives, as opposed to what we don't.

Emotional intelligence is an attribute that can generally be sustained and strengthened within each one of us, yet without having a created feeling of it, the people will need adoring fellowships, inner happiness, and for the most part, be consigned to carrying on with a life of low friendly working. Getting more aware of the effects and differences of EQ and IQ frequently causes us to accept that EQ is adequately more significant than one is general intelligence in light of the fact that being consistent with oneself is the most effortless method of making every moment count. In this worldwide age, it is important to gather a high feeling of emotional awareness. Who needs to carry on with a miserable life with not having the option to impart everything to the one we love?

No one at any point suggested getting automated or giving up your emotions in the work environment. Indeed, to be an extraordinary pioneer, you should be a human and one who has dominated emotional intelligence abilities.

Keep in mind, you need to channel your emotions to drive things and individuals forward instead of moving diverted yourself. As a pioneer, you need to continually seek after self-improvement and outfit your colleagues' capability to accomplish greater objectives.

You need to go through emotional intelligence ability building if you need to make progress in your work and in life. The individuals who understand the estimation of emotional intelligence ability's significance will make a solid effort to create them. They understand that they can assume responsibility for their lives by viably utilizing emotional intelligence and accomplishing their objectives. Such individuals don't move away from tolerating and seeking after some random undertaking. They continually center on creating emotional intelligence abilities and ultimately end up being extraordinary guides to other people who wish to dominate abilities to create emotional intelligence and have incredible existences!

# PART 2

# Mental Models

*The Ultimate Guide to Improve Your Mind. Learn Effective Problem-Solving and Critical Thinking Strategies to Finally Develop Logical Analysis and Decision-Making Skills.*

**Jennet Brown**

# Introduction

A conceptual model is a description of how someone thinks about how something functions in real life. It is a reflection of the surrounding universe, its different components, and a person's intuitive understanding of his or her own actions and consequences. Mental models can help form behavior and solve problems and complete tasks (similar to a personal algorithm).

A mental model is an inner symbol or image of external reality that has been linked to perception, reasoning, and decision-making. In 1943, Kenneth Craik proposed that the mind creates "small-scale versions" of reality that it uses to predict events. Human thought, according to one perspective, is based on conceptual templates. According to this viewpoint, mental models can be created by perception, imagination, or discourse comprehension (Johnson-Laird, 1983). In contrast to, say, the structure of logical forms used in formal rule theories of reasoning, such mental models are similar to architects' models or physicists' diagrams. Their structure is identical to the structure of the situation they represent. In this way, they resemble the pictures described by philosopher Ludwig Wittgenstein in his 1922 picture theory of language. Philip Johnson-Laird and Ruth M.J. Byrne introduced the mental model theory of reasoning, which assumes that reasoning is based on mental models rather than logical structure (Johnson-Laird and Byrne, 1991).

Mental models are distinguished from other proposed representations in the psychology of reasoning by a small collection of basic assumptions (axioms) (Byrne and Johnson-Laird, 2009). Every conceptual model represents a potential outcome. A conceptual model is a representation of one possibility that captures what is common to all of the possible outcomes (Johnson-Laird and Byrne, 2002). Mental models are iconic, meaning that each component of the model corresponds to a component of its representation (Johnson-Laird, 2006). Mental models are based on the theory of truth: they usually represent only possible situations, and each model of a possibility represents only what is true in that possibility according to the proposition. On the other hand, mental models may reflect what is false but is temporarily believed to be true, as in counterfactual conditionals and counterfactual thought (Byrne, 2005).

# Chapter 1 What Are Mental Models and How Do They Work?

We perceive the world by mental models. They influence not only what we think and how we view things, but also the links and opportunities we see. We use mental models to simplify uncertainty, explain why certain items are more important than others, and reason.

Simply put, a conceptual model is a description of how something works. Since we can't hold all of the details of the universe in our heads, we use templates to break down the complex into manageable chunks.

## Learning to Think More Critically

The utility of our mental models in the situation at hand is proportional to the consistency of our reasoning. The larger your toolbox of models, the more likely you are to have the right models for seeing life. It turns out that diversity is important when it comes to improving your decision-making abilities.

The majority of us, on the other hand, are experts. We have a few mental templates from our discipline instead of a latticework. Each expert sees things differently. A typical Engineer would think in systems by default. A counsellor can think in terms of rewards and punishments. A biologist can think in evolutionary terms. We can walk around a problem in three dimensions by combining these disciplines in our heads. We have a blind spot if we just look at the dilemma one way. Blind spots, on the other hand, can be fatal.

Here's another way to see it: When a botanist examines a forest, he or she might be interested in the habitat, an environmentalist in the effects of climate change, a forestry engineer in the state of tree growth, and a businessperson in the land value. None of them are incorrect, but none of them are capable of describing the forest in its entirety. Sharing expertise or studying the fundamentals of other disciplines will result in a more well-rounded understanding, allowing for better initial forest management decisions.

"Well, the first rule is that you can't really know much if you only recall isolated facts and try to bang 'em back," Charlie Munger said in a popular speech in the 1990s, summarizing the path to practical knowledge by knowing mental models. You don't functionally have evidence if they don't fit together on a latticework of theory. You must have mental templates in your brain. And you'll have to arrange your virtual and direct experiences on this latticework of models. You may have noticed students who simply want to recall and repeat what they have learned. They fail in school and in life, to be sure. You must hang your experience on a latticework of mental models."

## Mental Models in a Latticework

We've gathered and summarized the ones we've found the most helpful to help you construct your latticework of mental models so you can make better decisions.

Also, keep in mind that latticework is a lifetime project. If you stick with it, you'll notice that the ability to comprehend facts, make consistently wise decisions, and assist those you care about will continue to improve.

## Concepts in General Thinking

### 1. The map does not reflect the territory.

Truth is not depicted on a globe. Also the best maps have flaws. This is due to the fact that they are dilutions of what they portray. If a map accurately depicted the territory, it would no longer be a reduction, and therefore would no longer be useful to us. A map may also depict something that no longer exists, such as a snapshot of a moment in time. This is important to remember as we solve challenges and make better choices.

### 2. Competency Circle

We have blind spots when our actions are guided by ego rather than competence. If you know what you're talking about, you'll be able to see that you have an advantage over others. You'll know where you're insecure and where you can change if you're truthful about where your expertise is lacking. Understanding your circle of expertise helps you make better decisions and achieve better results.

### 3. Thinking from the Ground Up

One of the most effective ways to reverse-engineer complex situations and unleash imaginative potential is to use first principles thinking. It's a tool for helping to explain complex situations by separating the underlying concepts or evidence from any conclusions based on them. It's also known as reasoning from first principles. All that's left are the basics. If you understand the fundamentals of something, you can use the rest of your experience to create something different.

## 4. Experiment with your thoughts

"Devices of the imagination used to explore the essence of things" are how thought experiments are described. Thinking experiments are used in many fields, including philosophy and physics, to test what can be learned. They will be capable to open up new avenues for investigation and discovery as a result of this. Thought experiments are effective because they enable us to learn from our mistakes and avoid repeating them in the future. They allow us to take on the seemingly impossible, assess the possible repercussions of our actions, and revisit history in order to make better decisions. They will assist us in determining what we really want and the best route to get there.

## 5. Thinking in Second-Order

Almost everybody is able to predict the immediate consequences of their behavior. This style of first-order thinking is convenient and secure, but it also ensures that you get the same outcomes as anyone else. Second-order analysis entails planning ahead and seeing the big picture. It allows us to understand our immediate actions and their consequences and the long-term consequences of those actions. Failure to understand second and third order effects can have disastrous consequences.

## 6. Probabilistic Consideration

Probabilistic reasoning entails attempting to estimate the probability of a given outcome occurring using mathematical and logical methods. It is one of the most effective resources we have for increasing the precision of our decisions. Probabilistic reasoning aids us in identifying the possible outcomes in a world where an infinitely complex collection of factors decides each moment. When we have this information, we can make more accurate and successful decisions.

## 7. Reversal

Since it helps you recognize and eliminate barriers to success, inversion is a powerful tool for improving your thought. Inversion comes from the word "invert," which means "to upend or turn upside down." It means approaching a situation from the opposite end of the natural starting point as a thinking tool. Most of us have a tendency to approach a dilemma in one direction: forward. Inversion helps one to think backward by turning the dilemma around. Starting at the beginning is often beneficial, but starting at the end may be more beneficial.

## 8. The Rule of Occam's Razor

Simpler theories are more likely to be correct than those that are more complex. This is the core of Occam's Razor, a well-known logic and problem-solving theory. Rather than spending time attempting to disprove complicated scenarios, you will make more confident decisions by relying on the theory with the fewest moving pieces.

## Hanlon's Razor (number 9)

Hanlon's Razor, which has an enigmatic basis, notes that we can not assign to malice what is more readily explained by ignorance. This model helps us escape fear and ideology in a dynamic world. We search for alternatives instead of losing chances by not believing that poor outcomes are the product of a bad actor. This model serves as a reminder that people make mistakes. It begs the question of whether there is any plausible explanation for what has happened. The reason with the least amount of motive is the most likely to be right.

## 14 Mental Models to Get You Started (and Avoid)

### Theorem of Bayes

Based on potentially relevant factors, this describes the likelihood of something occurring. These considerations include data from previous results as well as existing circumstances that could have an effect on a new result.

Consider how this theorem might be applied in the marketing industry. Imagine you launched a four-month-old email marketing campaign with a 20% open rate. You conducted a similar email marketing campaign the following month with a 20% open rate target, but instead got a 25% open rate. Your email campaign had a 26% open rate in the third month. Then, last month, you removed your mailing list of contacts who hadn't opened an email from your company in the previous 60 days, and started another email campaign as a result.

Given your consistent rise in open rate over the last four months and the fact that you removed your most inactive emails from your contact list, a reasonable open rate target under Bayes' Theorem could be 30%.

## 2. Competency Circle

This mental model can be credited to Warren Buffett. Buffett told his shareholders in 1996, "You don't have to know everything about every company, or even a lot of them. You just need to be able to assess businesses within your area of expertise. The size of that circle is unimportant; however, knowing its boundaries is critical."

## Bias is a third factor to consider.

This is a natural human propensity to seek out and interpret evidence supporting or strengthening what you already believe.

For example, suppose you're optimistic that your website's organic traffic in December will surpass that in November. In that case, you may be focusing too much on December's promising traffic level after only the first week, and not enough on the fact that B2B website traffic sometimes decreases later in December due to the holidays.

Accept the idea that your perception does not always (or even frequently) equal reality to protect yourself from confirmation bias. Try to come up with various explanations about what's going on.

You may think in the example above, "Is there any reason to believe that our organic traffic for December will decrease before the end of the month? What obstacles could we face on our way to achieving our goal?"

Being more skeptical will cause you to dig deeper for objections, allowing you to set more reasonable goals before it's too late.

## 4. Mental Model of Inversion

One of the strongest mental models is the inversion viewpoint. Consider the result you'd like to stop rather than the one you'd like to achieve.

Let's say you want to advance to the role of senior marketing manager. Ask yourself, "What are the top 10 obstacles that would hinder my promotion?" instead of

"What are the top five things I should do to get promoted?"

Then you'd make sure you didn't do any of them.

"Avoiding stupidity is simpler than finding brilliance," Shane Parrish says. You won't always get the answer by inverting the issue, but you'll get better at it.

## 5. Fundamental Error in Attribution

We're more likely to believe someone's behavior is due to their personality rather than the circumstances.

In summary, if your social media strategist fails to show up for a marketing team meeting, you're more likely to think "They're flaky," rather than "They must have gotten stuck in traffic."

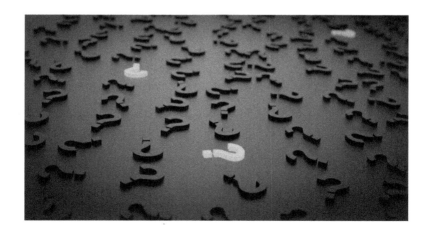

Give people the benefit of the doubt as much as you can. Because behavior is usually situational, you'll be more accurate in your predictions of how people will act if you don't blame it on "how they are."

Hanlon's Razor is number six.

You're probably going to assume that if a marketing qualified lead (MQL) goes silent at a critical point in the acquisition process, they were "kicking tires" or decided that the information they had wasn't good enough to continue the conversation. "Never attribute to malice what could be explained by carelessness," says Hanlon's Razor. To put it another way, it's more realistic to assume the person is preoccupied.

## 7. Jealousy Predisposition

Envy can be divided into two types. "Inferiority," or the desire to rise to the level of another person, is the productive type. Do you aspire to be as successful as the marketing director of your team? This kind of envy fuels your motivation.

On the other hand, Malicious envy is the desire to take something valuable from someone else, not for your own benefit, but so they don't have it.

When writing website copy for your online visitors, for example, keep these motivators in mind. Your visitors may be personally invested in a goal because they want to perform as well as — or better than — another employee at their company, or beat a previous record. Identifying your visitors' desires will aid you in writing landing page copy that addresses their specific needs.

You should also be aware of the tendency to be jealous in your own decision-making. A competitive streak (inferiority envy) may be advantageous in a fast-paced startup, but wanting other people to fail (malicious envy) will only serve to distract you. Avoid the temptation to sabotage them by reminding yourself of your similarities to this person, which will trigger your empathy. Turn your impulses into opportunities for growth: What skill or habit can you develop to achieve their outcomes?

## The Law of Diminishing Returns (Law of Diminishing Returns)

The progressive benefits you get from an investment get smaller and smaller after a certain point. You might lose six pounds in the first month of a diet, for example. You might lose three pounds in the second month. You might lose two pounds in the third month.

This idea can be applied to marketing in a variety of ways. First, make sure you're concentrating on the most important tasks. Let's pretend you spent a week researching your buyer persona before starting a blog just for them. Know when to call your buyer persona complete, as important as it is to your business. Passing another week sizing up your ideal buyer is unlikely to double your results, and the more trivial the details become, the less beneficial they are to your content. Instead, put that time to good use by researching a new buyer and creating multiple audience segments.

Identify what you need to know to be successful so you can spend your time on the things that will give you the most returns. Mastering the entire AP stylebook cover to cover might be more productive than developing a brand voice and a series of calls-to-actions for your blog.

Memorizing obscure details has diminishing returns, and the sooner you notice them, the sooner you can move on to projects that is more important to your company's growth.

### 9. The Safety Margin

Although a bridge could theoretically support 15,000 pounds, it would be prudent to set the weight limit at

14,000. If the bridge wasn't actually that strong, it would be a major disaster — and the risk isn't worth it.

The concept of a margin of safety is that we should leave ourselves some leeway in case we make a mistake or fail. For example, you might not count a downloaded ebook as a lead until they've responded to a follow-up email or requested more information from you when creating your website's conversion goals, just in case they change their minds.

Consider this model a safety net. It's preferable to be surprised than to be proven wrong.

Occam's razor is number ten.

The more basic explanation is usually the correct one, according to this principle. Develop the most basic hypothesis possible if you're trying to figure out what happened.

## 11 Opportunity Costs

Every decision is made at the expense of another. You won't be able to write a blog post if you decide to send emails after lunch. You won't have the bandwidth or risk tolerance to pursue another large, unpredictable lead-generation campaign at the same time if you focus on one.

Always keep this in the back of your mind when making decisions. What are your options? Are you desiring to let go of that?

## 12 The Pareto Principle

The Pareto Principle, also famous as the 80/20 rule, states that most outcomes are not evenly distributed. In other words, 20% of the work yields 80% of the results, 20% of your traffic yields 80% of your leads, 20% of features are responsible for 80% of your usage, and 20% of your time yields 80% of your results.

You'll be much more successful if you can focus on your top customers, selling activities, and so on.

For example, at my previous company, we analyzed our customers and discovered that those who spent the most (i.e., the 20% who generated 80% of our revenue) worked in HR. Our marketing and sales teams were able to target HR professionals once we knew that. The company's revenue increased by 230 percent as a result.

## 13 Preferential Attachment

Consider a race between two runners. Water and a protein bar are given to the first runner to cross the one-mile mark. The slower one gets nothing.

This is the preferred attachment, in which the leader is given more resources than his or her competitors. They have an even greater advantage because of those resources.

This effect can be seen in the lead-nurturing process as a marketer. It's easy to get caught up in the temptation of spending all of your time serving content to your most qualified leads. However, you may overlook those who are just starting to learn about your company, or you may take a little longer to open their emails and download certain resources.

It's important not to develop privileged attachment to your furthest-along leads at the expense of other website visitors, no matter how much you "prefer" getting your furthest-along leads into the hands of a salesperson.

## 14. Deficiency

Redundancy explains what good engineers do to put back-up systems in place to protect against failure in a similar way. This significantly lowers the odds of complete failure.

As a marketer, you can use this strategy to create a campaign that keeps your readers, subscribers, leads, and existing customers happy and informed while also taking a chance on a new product. Perhaps you're currently promoting a large product and have a lofty lead-generation target for next month. Pursue four or five smaller, low-risk content campaigns at once to keep your lead-gen pipeline stable while also launching your new product.

First and foremost, before we get into how mental models can completely transform your career, let's define what mental models are: ideas, "tools, principles, and perceptions that we consistently use to solve better decisions or understand life," Thomas Oppong explains. As a result, every principle...that we use in our daily lives, whether in business, career, or life, can be classified as mental models."

**So, that point of view we were talking about earlier, the one that gives you a unique perspective on the world?** Consider it your mental model. There are, however, other mental models (or lenses through which you can view things) that you can apply to specific situations to gain a deeper level of understanding and insight than you could get from your personal experience. As a result, you'll be able to make better decisions and solve problems more quickly.

As an example, I'll use myself. I'm a writer with a good command of the English language (if I do say so myself). But what about the numbers? Not at all. So, if I had to figure out how much I need to save each month in order to retire comfortably in 30+ years based solely on my own background and experience, I wouldn't know where to start ($50 a month, cross my fingers, and hope for the best?)

But, thankfully, I don't have to look at the problem through my own personal lens; there's a mental model for that!

Compounding is a mental model that can be used to calculate how much interest will accrue over a specific period of time when applied to investment situations (such as retirement).

So, instead of slapping my head against a brick wall, I can use the compounding mental model to figure out how much to set aside each month, and voila! The issue of retirement planning has been resolved.

Mental models are simply explanations of how things work.

They direct our thinking by providing us with "lenses" or formulas that we might not have had access to before, which we can use to boost our problem-solving abilities and make decision-making easier and faster. "Mental models have a lot to offer... so many people have experimented with different ways to make things better, different ways to make better decisions," Oppong explains. They've then passed on these principles and ideas to the rest of us.

As people continue to find and apply mental models in their daily lives, [mental models] shorten the decision-making process and make it easier for us to do better, make better assumptions, and make better decisions."

Mental models can facilitate us think beyond our own personal experience and provide a mental "shortcut" that makes finding solutions to problems easier, faster, and more efficient.

## What Is The Relationship Between Mental Models, Productivity, And Achievement?

So now that you understand what mental models are, let's talk about how they work—and how they relate to your career, success, and productivity in particular.

**Mental models can help you increase your productivity, get more done, and advance in your career in a variety of ways, including:**

• Reducing the amount of time spent solving problems. Consider what it would be like if you had to start from scratch to solve every problem you encountered throughout the day. You can more quickly and easily comprehend the problem at hand—and, more importantly, arrive at the best and most productive solution—by using mental models.

• Introducing new and different ways of thinking to your mind. As previously stated, we each have our own distinct way of looking at things, but that distinct way of looking at things can sometimes hold us back. You can take out yourself from the equation and approach things from a more objective standpoint by using mental models. And what about that willingness to broaden your horizons and see things from a different perspective? It's essential for personal and professional development.

"Once you're open to learning [and trying out different mental models], you'll be able to identify your own biases, traps, and mental biases that are preventing you from progressing," says Oppong.

• Assisting you in becoming more adaptable. People who can roll with the punches and adapt to changing circumstances are the most successful. The more mental models you grasp, the more you'll be able to see things from various angles—and the more adaptable and flexible you'll be when solving problems.

## Mental Models That Can Assist You In Moving Your Career Forward

Mental models are something you're familiar with. You're aware of how they can help you work more efficiently. Let's look at the specific mental models you'll need to succeed in your career now.

### The Competence Circle

Warren Buffet created the circle of mental competence model, which was originally used to guide investment decisions but is now extremely relevant to business.

The areas in which you excel are known as your circle of competence. You should stay within that circle at all times. You won't be as effective if you try to break out of that circle (and focus on tasks about which you have little knowledge or experience), and your productivity will suffer as a result.

**Farnam Street is the source of this information.**

Assume you're the CEO of a startup, and your circle of competence includes things like pitching investors, mentoring your team, and devising long-term strategies.

If you want your business to succeed, you should focus your efforts there; if you focus on tasks outside of your area of expertise (for example, managing budgets or writing social media copy), your productivity will suffer— and your startup will suffer as well.

Take the time to figure out who belongs in your circle of competence. Consider the following questions: • What am I good at? • What do I enjoy doing? • Where do I excel?

Then devote your time and energy to it—and figure out how to eliminate the tasks that fall outside of your area of expertise (for example, by hiring an assistant).

## Monetary incentives (AKA Reward and Punishment)

All living things (including humans) are inherently incentive-driven, according to the incentives mental model—once you understand this principle, you can apply it to your work and incentivize yourself to get things done.

Is there a task on your to-do list that you worry about every day, for example? If you respond better to positive incentives (or rewards), you could tell yourself things like, "If I finish XYZ task by 12pm, I can have an iced coffee for lunch."

If you're more motivated by negative incentives (a.k.a. punishment), you could tell yourself, "If I don't finish XYZ task by 12pm, no iced coffee with lunch today."

In either case, the reward or punishment will provide the motivation you need to complete your dreaded work task, making it easier to complete and increasing your productivity.

## Framework for Reducing Regret

The regret minimization framework comes into play when the choice that offers immediate gratification isn't always the right or most efficient.

"The Regret Minimization Framework is another [mental model] that I've found to be really helpful," says Oppong.

The regret minimization system, created by Amazon CEO Jeff Bezos, encourages you to look beyond the current moment and helps you make the right decision for your future.

"Whenever you take action, instead of focusing on what will benefit you in the short term, you concentrate on what will benefit you in the long term," Oppong explains. Long term, not only the next five or ten years, but the next fifteen or twenty."

This mental model provides you with a structure for assessing your choices and how they can affect your long-term success and well-being.

So, for example, you are given a promotion at work, but it will necessitate you working longer hours. You could be tempted to say no if you were just thinking about the short-term gain (who wants to work late when there's Netflix to watch?!). However, by using the regret minimization framework, you can determine how the decision will affect you in the long run and realize that, in ten years, you'll actually regret passing up a promotion for more time with your Netflix queue.

The law of Diminishing Returns is described as "the point in which the level of income or benefits earned is less than the amount of money or energy invested"—you can use this mental model to boost your productivity and ensure you're getting the most bangs for your buck. This law is a principle that states that as time goes on,

What is the secret to effectively applying the rule of diminishing returns?

Identify the "point" where the cost of energy outweighs the profit and ensures that you work up to, but never past, that point.

Here's a perfect illustration of the rule of diminishing returns in action: The number of hours a day that you work.

Everyone reaches a point where the juice is no longer worth the squeeze, where they are theoretically "working," but their minds are so drained that they are unable to complete tasks.

Identifying the time of day when you reach that point—and working before then, but not a minute after—will help you improve your productivity on a daily basis (without veering into burnout territory).

## Mindsets: Fixed and Growing

According to this mental model, there are two ways to see you, which was pioneered by Stanford psychologist and researcher Carol S. Dweck in her book Mindset. If you have a fixed or development mentality.

You assume who you are, including your skills, strengths, and abilities, is set in stone if you have a fixed mentality. You're who you're supposed to be, right? Nothing is going to change.

The idea that the skills, strengths, and abilities are continually improving is known as a growth mindset. Change and, as the name suggests, development are often possibilities.

## Chapter 2 Types of mental model? And how it works?

### The Pareto Principle, What is and How Does It Work?

The Pareto Principle states that 80% of the results come from 20% of the causes, implying an unequal relationship between inputs and outputs. It was named after renowned economist Vilfredo Pareto. This concept acts as a general reminder that the input-output relationship is unbalanced. The Pareto Principle, also known as the Pareto Rule or the 80/20 Rule, is a mathematical principle.

### Essential

• According to the Pareto Principle, 80% of the consequences result from 20% of the causes.

• Unlike other values, the Pareto Principle was derived from an inequality in land ownership in Italy, and is widely used to demonstrate the notion that not all things are equal, and the minority controls the majority. Despite its broad use, it does not apply to every situation.

75% of total volume

2:00:23

The Pareto Principle is a set of regulations that governs how much of (80-20 Rule)

The Pareto Principle: What It Is and What It Isn't

The Pareto Principle was first observed in relation to the relationship between wealth and population. According to Pareto, 20 percent of the population owned 80 percent of the land in Italy. After surveying a number of other nations, he discovered that the same was true there as well. The Pareto Principle is, for the most part, an assertion that things in existence are not necessarily distributed equally.

Manufacturing, administration, and human resources are all fields where the Pareto Principle can be implemented. For example, the efforts of 20% of a company's employees might account for 80% of the company's income. The Pareto Principle is particularly useful in client-service-oriented businesses. A number of coaching and customer relationship management (CRM) software systems have incorporated it.

It can be used on a personal level as well. The Pareto Principle is most often used in time management since most people prefer to thinly spread out their time rather than concentrating on the most critical tasks. In terms of personal time management, only 20% of your time at work will produce 80% of your work-related productivity.

**The Pareto Principle in Action**

Financial consulting firms often use the Pareto Principle to handle their clients. The advisor's ability to deliver outstanding customer support is critical to the company's success, as its fees are based on customer satisfaction. However, not every client pays the counselor the same amount of money. According to the Pareto Principle, if an investment practice has 100 clients, the top 20 clients can account for 80% of the financial advisor's revenue. These 20 clients have the most assets and are paying the highest fees.

The Pareto Principle seems plain, but it is difficult to put into practice for the average financial advisor. According to the philosophy, since 20 clients pay 80% of the total payments, they should expect at least 80% of the customer support. As a result, advisors should devote the majority of their time to maintaining relationships with their top 20 clients.

This, however, does not occur, as human nature implies. Most advisors distribute their time and resources based on the position of their clients. If a client calls with a problem, the counselor handles it appropriately, regardless of how much money the client brings in.

As a result of this theory, advisors are focusing on replicating their top 20% of clients, recognizing that adding a client of that size has an immediate impact on the bottom line.

## The Pareto Principle's Benefits

The Pareto Principle is useful for a number of reasons. Simply put, it will help you figure out how to reward and what to fix. For example, if 20% of a car's design flaws cause 80% of the accidents, those flaws can be identified and fixed. Similarly, if 20% of your customers account for 80% of your revenue, you can pay special attention to them and thank them for their loyalty. In this way, the Pareto Principle serves as a template for effectively allocating resources.

## The Pareto Principle's Drawbacks

Although Pareto's observation is correct, this does not necessarily imply that it is always correct. For example, 30% of the workforce (or 30 out of 100 employees) can only complete 60% of the job. The remaining employees may not be as effective or may simply be slackers. This emphasizes that the Pareto Principle is merely an intuition rather than a rule.

## What Is The 80/20 Rule, and How Does It Work?

The 80/20 rule is also known as the "Pareto Principle," as I stated earlier. It was founded in 1895 and named after its founder, the Italian economist Vilfredo Pareto. He observed that people in society seemed to naturally divide into the "vital few," or the top 20% in terms of wealth and power, and the "trivial many," or the bottom 80%.

Later, he found that nearly all economic activity was governed by this theory, with 20% of the population controlling 80% of the resources in Italy at the time.

Pareto's 80/20 rule can be applied to almost any case. Understanding the theory is key to learning how to prioritize your tasks, days, weeks, and months.

It's critical to strategic planning in business, and it's one of the leadership qualities shared by the world's most powerful leaders.

## How Does the Pareto Principle Work?

The Pareto Principle is a philosophy that assumes two out of ten items, on any general to-do list, would turn out to be worth more than the other eight items added together.

The sad truth is that most people procrastinate on the top 10 or 20 percent of things that are the most valuable and interesting and busy themselves instead with the least important 80 percent, that contribute scarcely to their success.

**Goal Setting: How To Apply the 80 20 Rule**

Here's what you can do in order to successfully apply the 80/20 rule to setting SMART goals which will improve your overall productivity.

First, write down ten targets. Then ask yourself: If you could only achieve one of the goals on that list today, which one goal will have the greatest positive effect on your life?

Then pick the second most important target. What you'll notice that, once you complete this exercise, you will have determined the most significant 20 percent of your objectives that will motivate you more than anything else.

Keep working at those goals that you've selected as the most important all the time.

## Eat the Biggest Frog First

You also see people who seem to be busy all day long but manage to achieve very little. Most of the time they are busy focusing on low importance projects while they are procrastinating on the one or two activities that could make a huge difference to their businesses and their careers.

The most important things you can perform each day are always the hardest and most complicated, but the payoff and rewards for completing them can be enormous.

Always ask yourself about work, "Is this job in the top 20 percent of my tasks or in the bottom 80 percent?"

The rule for this is: avoid the urge to clear up little items first.

If you want to start your day working on low-value tasks, you will soon grow the habit of still beginning and working on low-value tasks.

## Achieve Success In Life using the Pareto Rule

The starting point of great success and accomplishment has always been the same.

It starts with you dreaming big dreams.

Nothing more necessary, and nothing that works faster than for you to throw off your own limitations than for you to begin dreaming and fantasizing about the wonderful things you will become, have, and do.

"You must dream great dreams, for only big dreams have the power to move the minds of men" a wise man once said. When you begin to dream big dreams, the levels of self-esteem and self-confidence will go up automatically. You can feel more powerful about yourself and your ability to cope with what happens to you. So many people do so little because they never allow themselves to lean back and envision the kind of life that is possible for them.

## Theory of Constraints

An important philosophy that you can use to dream big dreams and live without limitations is found in what Elihu Goldratt calls the "Theory of Constraints." This is one of the biggest breakthroughs in modern thinking. What Goldratt has found is that there is a bottleneck or choke cord in any process in accomplishing every target, which acts as a restriction on the process. This limit then determines the pace at which you reach some specific target.

Goldratt noticed that if you focus all of your creative energy and attention on alleviating the limitation, you can speed up the process faster than by doing some other single thing.

Let me give you an example. Let us assume that you want to double your salary. What is the vital restriction or the limiting factor that holds you back? Well, you know that your salary is a direct reward for the quality and quantity of the services you provide to your world. Whatever sector you are in, if you want to double your income, you literally have to double the quality and quantity of what you do for that income. Always ask yourself, "What is the vital restriction that holds me back or sets the pace on how fast I double my income?"

### The 80 20 Rule In Action

One of the highest-paid commission practitioners in the United States is a friend of mine. One of his targets was to double his income over the next three to five years.

He applied the 80 20 law to his client base.

What he noticed was that 20 percent of his clients contributed 80 percent of his earnings. He also noticed that the amount of time spent on a high-profit client was pretty much the same amount of time spent on a low-profit client.

In other words, he was splitting his time evenly over the number of things that he does although just 20 percent of those items led to 80 percent of his performance.

So he took his list of clients and drew a line under those that represented the top 20 percent and then called in other professionals in his industry and very carefully, respectfully, and strategically handed off the 80 percent of his clients who only represented 20 percent of his company.

He then set a profile of his top clients and started searching in the marketplace specifically for the type of client that matched the profile; in other words, one who could become a significant benefit contributor to his company, and whom he in turn could represent with the degree of quality that his clients were accustomed to. And instead of doubling his income in three to five years, he doubled it in the first year with that one easy time management strategy!

**Identify the Limitations to Your Productivity**

Most people will usually recognize a few obstacles between them and their objectives. They have often acquired feelings of helplessness. It's not uncommon for them to be nothing more than excuses.

Then, what's stopping you? Is it your level of education or competence that's the issue?

What else stands in your path if your ambition is to be a published author and you learn how to write a book using an established system?

Is it your new employment or occupation? Is it your current living situation or your current state of health? Is it because of the circumstances you're in right now? What determines how quickly you achieve your goal?

Remember that you can undo everything you've learned. You will usually pull yourself out of whatever situation you've found yourself in. If your true ambition is to achieve big dreams and live without boundaries, you can use this as a benchmark and measure everything you do against it.

**The Three Keys to Living without Boundaries**

There have always been three keys to living a life without boundaries. Clarity, integrity, and concentration are three of them.

## #1: Make Your Desires, Goals, and Vision Clearly Definable

You are completely straightforward on who you are, what you want, and where you're going if you have clarity. You write down your objectives and make preparations to achieve them. You set very clear targets and do something every day to help you achieve your objectives. And the more progress you make in achieving your goals, the more self-confidence and self-belief you gain, and the more confident you are that there are no limits to what you can accomplish.

Having a clear understanding of your desires and a clear vision for your future will help you remain focused on your objectives every day. Focusing on your goals on a regular basis is, in my view, one of the most critical behaviors of successful people.

**This is why:**

Those who set goals on a regular basis have more clarity and achievement in life than those who do not. They're much more likely to be conscious of their time management and interested in optimization strategies like the Pareto Principle.

## # 2: Expertise in Your Focused Areas

Competence entails being extremely proficient in your chosen field's main outcome areas. You follow the 80/20 rule with everything you do and concentrate on excelling at the 20% of activities that lead to 80% of your success. You make it a point to keep learning new things. It is impossible to avoid rising. You understand that perfection is a moving goal. And you make a daily commitment to do something that will help you get better at doing the most important things in your career.

## Concentration is number three

Concentration is described as having the self-discipline to focus solely on one thing, the most important thing, and to stick with it until it is completed.

Focus and concentration have always been the two main terms for performance.

Knowing just what you want to be, have, and do is the definition of focus. Concentration is the ability to persevere in a straight line, without interruption or distraction, toward achieving the goals that will make a real difference in your life.

Allowing yourself to start dreaming big dreams, creatively abandoning things that are taking up so much of your time and focusing your inner energy on alleviating your key constraints gives you an immense sense of strength and trust. You begin to think about possibilities rather than impossibilities as you concentrate on doing what you enjoy and being outstanding in the few areas that can make a real difference in your life, and you step closer to realizing your full potential.

**Always have the main goal in mind.**

Finally, I'd like to share with you the results of a recent study comparing the attitudes of rich and poor people toward target setting. They discovered that 85 percent of wealthy people have a single major target that they are constantly pursuing.

Confirmation bias is a type of cognitive bias that occurs when people

Confirmation bias is the propensity to process evidence by seeking out or interpreting data that supports one's pre-existing beliefs. This skewed approach to decision-making is largely accidental, and it often leads to the omission of contradictory data. Expectations in a given situation and assumptions regarding a specific result are examples of existing beliefs. When the subject is highly critical or self-relevant, people are more likely to filter knowledge to support their own views.

Confirmation bias is an example of how humans can interpret knowledge in an illogical and biased way. Many variables, many of which people are unaware of, may have an impact on how information is processed. According to philosophers, humans have trouble processing information in a logical, impartial manner once they have formed an opinion about a problem. Suppose they are emotionally removed from the problem. In that case, humans are better able to rationally process knowledge, giving equal weight to different perspectives (although a low level of confirmation bias can still occur when an individual has no vested interests).

It is an efficient way of processing information, which may explain why humans are prone to confirmation bias. In the social environment, humans are bombarded with knowledge and cannot possibly take the time to properly process each piece of data in order to reach an impartial conclusion. Since people are restricted to viewing information from their own point of view, human decision-making and information analysis are often skewed. To protect themselves from injury, people must process information quickly. Relying on instinctive, automatic reflexes to keep humans out of harm's way is adaptive.

People also use confirmation bias to protect their self-esteem. People like to feel good about them, so learning that a deeply held belief is incorrect makes they feel bad about themselves. As a result, people will seek out information that confirms their current beliefs. Another motivation is precision. People want to believe they are smart, and information that suggests they have an incorrect belief or made a poor decision suggests they are not.

**The Competence Circle**

The Circle of Competence concept is straightforward: Each of us has acquired useful knowledge in certain areas of the world through experience or study. Some areas are familiar to most of us, while others necessitate a higher level of expertise to assess.

Most of us, for example, have a basic understanding of restaurant economics: You rent or buy a location, spend money on furnishings, and then hire people to seat, serve, cook, and clean. (And manage if you don't want to do it yourself.)

After all of your operating expenses have been paid, it's just a matter of generating enough traffic and setting the appropriate prices to make a profit on the food and drinks you serve. Though each restaurant's cuisine, atmosphere, and price points will differ, they must all adhere to the same economic formula.

With that foundation, a basic understanding of accounting, and a little research, one could evaluate and invest in a variety of restaurants and restaurant chains, both public and private. It isn't all that difficult.

**Reasons why you should stick to your area of expertise**

**What method do you use to determine your circle of competence?**

For the most part, it begins with your own job or profession. Your profession provides you with an in-depth understanding of how your industry and the companies that make up your industry operate and function. When it comes to investing in your industry, knowing which companies are the best to pick out of the bunch and which ones are dead-in-the-water and must be avoided is extremely valuable.

How you spend your money is another way to determine your circle of competence. Suppose you are a knowledgeable consumer of any product or service you frequently use. In that case, you may have a good understanding of which companies are more likely to succeed with customers and thrive in any given market.

**There are three reasons why you should stick to your friends and family.**

1. You have a leg up on the competition in terms of knowledge. If you work as a property agent, you specialize in the real estate industry. You're more likely to understand how market sentiments influence property prices, where the best investment opportunities are, and how much a piece of land is really worth. For example, you could use information you have and invest in a company that owns a number of valuable real estate properties. The stock market may have undervalued the company's stock, selling it for less than its net tangible assets. You should concentrate your efforts on your given area of expertise because you have more knowledge and experience than others. You'll have a better chance of succeeding!

2. It reduces the number of stocks you can choose from. There are over 46,332 companies listed worldwide, according to the World Federation of Exchanges. With over 700 stocks to choose from in Singapore alone, I'm spoiled for choice. If I spent a month on each one, it would take me more than 58 years to complete the Singapore stock exchange! Because I was a specialist in aerospace engineering, I immediately looked at publicly traded companies that were in my field. I narrowed it down to two companies, SIA Engineering and ST Engineering, and I assessed their operations and got up to speed quickly.

3. You commit fewer errors. A friend of mine, one and a half years ago, shared with me an investment idea, Civmec Limited,. Civmec is primarily involved in the mining, oil, and gas industries, all of which I am unfamiliar with! Civmec's management was confident in the company's growth and that its share price would hit $2 and up due to the highly optimistic mining outlook in Australia, where the company is based. The stock was trading at $1.20 at the time, implying a potential upside of 66 percent. Unfortunately, its stock is now worth 75 cents, a 37.5 percent drop (fortunately for me!). I was able to avoid the bullet by staying within my circle of

competence. If you stick to something you know and understand, you'll make far fewer mistakes.

## Maslow's Needs Hierarchy

Maslow's hierarchy of needs is a psychological motivational theory that consists of a five-tier model of human needs, which is frequently depicted as hierarchical levels within a pyramid. Physiological (food and clothing), love, safety (job security) and belonging needs (friendship), esteem, and self-actualization are the needs from the bottom of the hierarchy up.

Individuals must attend to lower-level needs before they can attend to higher-level needs.

## Needs for deficiency vs. needs for growth

There are two types of needs in this five-stage model: deficiency and growth. Deficiency needs (D-needs) refer to the first four levels, while growth or being needs refers to the top level (B-needs).

Growth requirements arise from a desire to develop as a person, not from a lack of something. After these needs for growth have been met to a reasonable degree, one may be able to reach the highest level of self-actualization.

Every person has the desire and ability to progress up the hierarchy toward self-actualization. Unfortunately, failure to meet lower-level needs frequently stymies progress. Divorce and job loss are examples of life events that can cause a person to move up and down the hierarchy.

As a result, not everyone will progress through the hierarchy in a single direction, but instead will switch back and forth between the various types of needs.

The five stages of the initial hierarchy of needs model are as follows:

According to Maslow (1943, 1954), people are driven to meet some needs, and certain needs take priority over others.

Physical survival is our most basic need, and it will be the power behind our actions. When that level is concluded, we are motivated to move on to the next level, and so on.

1. Physiological needs - air, food, drink, shelter, clothing, warmth, sex, and sleep are all biological necessities for human survival.

The human body cannot act optimally if these needs are not met. Physiological needs are the most significant, according to Maslow, since all other needs are secondary before these are met.

2. Protection needs - Once a person's physiological needs are met, security and safety become more important. In their daily lives, people seek order, predictability, and power. These needs can be met by the family and community (e.g. police, schools, business and medical care).

Emotional security, financial security (e.g., work, social welfare), law and order, fearlessness, social stability, land, and health and wellbeing are just a few examples (e.g. safety against accidents and injury).

3. Needs for belonging and love - after physiological and protection needs are met, the third stage of human needs is psychological, which includes feelings of belonging. The need for interpersonal connections drives action.

Friendship, intimacy, confidence, acceptance, and receiving and giving affection and love are examples. Belonging to a club, affiliating (family, friends, work).

4. The fourth level of Maslow's hierarchy is confidence needs, which are divided into two categories: I self-esteem (dignity, accomplishment, mastery, independence) and (ii) the desire for others' reputation or appreciation (e.g., status, prestige).

According to Maslow, the need for respect or prestige is the most critical for children and adolescents, and it comes before true self-esteem or integrity.

Self-actualization is number five. The highest level in Maslow's hierarchy relates to a person's potential realization, self-fulfillment, personal development, and peak experiences. This level is described by Maslow (1943) as the desire to achieve anything one can, to become the best one can be.

This need can be perceived or focused on quite narrowly by individuals. One person, for example, will have a strong desire to be the perfect parent. In another, the desire can be manifested in terms of money, academics, or athletics. Others may express their feelings through art, such as paintings, photographs, or inventions.

Over the course of several decades, Maslow refined his theory based on the idea of a hierarchy of needs (Maslow, 1943, 1962, 1987).

Maslow (1987) suggested that the hierarchy's order is "not nearly as rigid" (p. 68) as he might have inferred in his earlier explanation.

The order of needs, according to Maslow, can be versatile depending on external circumstances or individual differences. For example, he states that the need for self-esteem is more critical for some people than the need for love. For others, the need to be innovative can outweigh even the most basic needs.

Maslow (1987) also observed that most behavior is multi-motivated, stating that "any behavior appears to be dictated by many or all of the basic needs at the same time rather than by only one" (p. 71).

## Hierarchy of requirements in conclusion

(a) A hierarchy of needs motivates human beings.

(b) Needs are arranged in a hierarchy of prepotency, with more specific needs having to be fulfilled in some way (rather than all or nothing) before higher needs can be met.

(c) The order of needs isn't set in stone, but can change depending on external factors or individual differences.

(d) Most action is multi-motivated, meaning many basic needs guide it at the same time.

## The new hierarchy of requirements

Maslow's (1943, 1954) five-stage model has been extended to include cognitive and aesthetic needs (Maslow, 1970a), as well as later transcendence needs (Maslow, 1970b).

A seven-stage model and an eight-stage model, both built during the 1960s and 1970s, are highlighted as modifications to the original five-stage model.

1. Biological and physiological requirements - oxygen, food, water, shelter, warmth, sex, sleep, and so on.

2. Needs for safety: protection from the elements, security, order, law, peace, and fearlessness.

3. Needs for love and belonging - friendship, intimacy, confidence, acceptance, and receiving and giving affection. Belonging to a club, affiliating (family, friends, work).

4. Self-esteem - Maslow divided self-esteem into two categories: (i) esteem for oneself (dignity, accomplishment, mastery, independence) and (ii) esteem for others (reputation or respect).

5. Cognitive requirements: intelligence and comprehension, interest, exploration, and the need for context and predictability.

6. Aesthetic requirements - appreciation and pursuit of elegance, harmony, and shape, among other things

7. Needs for self-actualization include understanding one's full potential, self-fulfillment, personal development, and peak experiences. A urge to "become everything one is capable of"

8. Transcendence requirements - A person is inspired by ideals that go beyond his or her own personal self.

## Realization of one's potential

Maslow (1943) developed a more optimistic account of human nature that concentrated on what goes right rather than psychopathology and what goes wrong with people. He was fascinated by human potential and how we can realize it.

According to psychologist Abraham Maslow (1943, 1954), human motivation is focused on people finding fulfillment and transformation through personal development. Self-actualized people are happy and accomplishing whatever they set out to do.

The desire for personal development and exploration that is present in a person's life is referred to as self-actualization (Maslow, 1962). According to Maslow, an individual is always 'becoming,' and never remains stagnant in these words. Self-actualization is when a person discovers a meaningful purpose in existence that is meaningful to them.

Since each person's motivation for self-actualization is different, people pursue it in different ways. Self-actualization can be accomplished in a variety of ways for different individuals. For others, it can be achieved through the creation of works of art or literature, and for others, it can be achieved through sports, in the classroom, or in the workplace.

Maslow (1962) claimed that peak perceptions could be used to assess self-actualization. When a person experiences the world fully for what it is, feelings of euphoria, excitement, and wonder arise.

It's important to remember that self-actualization is a never-ending process of growth rather than a perfect state of 'happily ever after' (Hoffman, 1988).

**The following is Maslow's definition of self-actualization:**

'It refers to a person's desire for self-fulfillment, specifically the tendency for him to become actualized in who he is.'

Of course, the exact form that these needs will take will differ greatly from one individual to the next. It may take the form of a desire to be an ideal mother in one person, athleticism in another, and drawing pictures or inventions in yet another (Maslow, 1943, p. 382–383).

Self-actualized individuals have those characteristics.

While we are all technically capable of self-actualization, the majority of us will not, or will only do so to a small extent. Just two percent of individuals, according to Maslow (1970), would achieve self-actualization.

He was particularly intrigued by the characteristics of people who, in his opinion, had realized their full potential as individuals.

Maslow (1970) described 15 characteristics of a self-actualized individual after observing 18 individuals he found to be self-actualized (including Abraham Lincoln and Albert Einstein).

**Self-actualizers have the following characteristics:**

1. They have a good sense of truth and can cope with confusion.

2. Accept themselves, as well as others, for who they are.

3. Thoughts and actions that is spontaneous.

4. Problem-oriented (rather than self-centered);

5. A peculiar sense of humor.

6. Having the ability to look at life objectively.

7. Incredibly inventive.

8. Resistant to enculturation, but not deliberately so.

9. Concerned for humanity's well-being.

Ten. Capable of a profound understanding of basic life experiences.

11th. Develop deep and rewarding interpersonal relationships with a select group of people.

12. Inventive+ phrasing Peak encounters.

13th. Privacy is required.

14th. Democratic viewpoints.

15th. Moral/ethical expectations are high.

**Self-actualization-promoting behavior:**

(a) Experiencing life through the eyes of a child, fully immersed and focused;

(b) Experimenting with new ideas rather than sticking to tried-and-true methods;

(c) When analyzing perceptions, listening to your own emotions rather than the voice of tradition, authority, or the majority;

(d) Being truthful and avoiding deception ('game playing').

(e) Expecting to be unpopular if your viewpoint differs from that of the majority;

f) Accepting responsibility and putting in long hours;

(g) Trying to figure out what your defenses are and finding the ability to let go of them.

The traits of self-actualizes, as well as the behaviors that contribute to self-actualization, are mentioned above. Despite the fact that everyone achieves self-actualization in their own particular way, there are certain characteristics that they all share. 'There are no complete human beings,' however, but self-actualization is a matter of degree (Maslow,1970a, p. 176).

It is not important to exhibit all 15 traits in order to be self-actualized, and not only self-actualized people can do so.

Maslow did not associate perfection with self-actualization. Self-actualization is nothing more than realising one's full potential. As a result, someone can be foolish, wasteful, vain, and impolite and still achieve self-actualization. Self-actualization is achieved by less than 2% of the population.

## Rogers' Self-Actualization Theory

### Educational applications

Maslow's (1962) hierarchy of needs theory has made a significant contribution to teaching and classroom management in schools. Rather than restricting action to a reaction in the environment, Maslow (1970a) adopts a holistic approach to education and learning.

Maslow looks at the complete physical, mental, social, and intellectual qualities of a person and how they impact on learning.

Applications of Maslow's hierarchy theory to the work of the classroom teacher are evident. Before a student's cognitive requirements can be met, they must first meet their basic physiological needs.

For example, a tired and hungry student would find it difficult to concentrate on learning. Students need to feel emotionally and physically secure and welcomed within the classroom to progress and achieve their full potential.

Maslow says students must be told that they are appreciated and respected in the classroom, and the teacher should build a welcoming atmosphere. Students with a low self-esteem will not advance academically at an optimal pace until their self-esteem is increased.

Maslow (1971, p. 195) concluded that a humanistic educational approach would produce people who are "stronger, healthier, and would take their own lives into their hands to a greater degree. With increased personal responsibility for one's personal life, and with a fair set of principles to direct one's choosing, people will begin to change the environment in which they lived consciously".

## A critical assessment

Maslow's theory has a number of flaws, the most significant of which is his methodology. Maslow used a qualitative method called biographical analysis to formulate the characteristics of self-actualized people.

He looked at the biographies and writings of 18 self-actualized individuals he named. He compiled a list of qualities that seemed to be unique to this group of people, as opposed to humanity as a whole, based on these sources.

From a theoretical perspective, there are a slew of issues with this approach. To begin with, it could be argued that biographical analysis as a method is extremely subjective because it is solely based on the researcher's opinion. Personal opinion is prone to bias, lowering the validity of any data gathered. As a result, Maslow's operational definition of self-actualization should not be taken at face value.

## Theory and Examples of Comparative Advantage

When a country offer a service or good for a lower opportunity cost than other countries, it is said to have comparative advantage. A trade-off is measured by opportunity cost. The trade-off is worth it for a country with a comparative advantage. The advantages of purchasing its product or service outweigh the drawbacks. It's possible that the country isn't the best at producing something. However, importing the product or service has a low opportunity cost for other nations. 1

Chemicals, for example, are a comparative advantage for oil-producing countries. Compared to countries without it, their locally generated oil provides a low-cost source of material for the chemicals. The oil distillery method produces a lot of the raw materials. As a result, Kuwait, Saudi Arabia and Mexico are able to compete with American chemical manufacturers. Their chemicals are cheap, so they have a low opportunity cost. 2

India's call centers are another example. Many businesses in the United States purchase this service because it is less expensive than finding a call center in the United States; however, many people experience miscommunication when dealing with Indian call centers due to language barriers. However, they provide the service at a low enough price to make the tradeoff worthwhile. 3

Comparative advantages were more common in products than in services in the past. This is due to the fact that goods are easier to export. However, telecommunications technology, such as the internet, is making it easier to export services. Call centers, banking, and entertainment are among the facilities available.

## Comparative Advantage Theory

Economist David Ricardo developed the theory of comparative advantage in the eighteenth century. He said that a country's economic growth is boosted the most by concentrating on the sector in which it has the greatest competitive advantage. 5

England, for example, was able to produce inexpensive fabric. Portugal had ideal conditions for producing low-cost wine. England would stop making wine, and Portugal would stop making fabric, according to Ricardo. He was absolutely right. Trading England's cloth for Portugal's wine, and vice versa, resulted in a greater profit for England. Since England lacked the climate, making all of the wine it needed would have been prohibitively expensive. Portugal lacked the manufacturing capability to produce low-cost fabric. As a result, by trading what they made most effectively, they both gained.

Free trade agreements were founded on the principle of comparative advantage.

In England, Ricardo developed his strategy to fight trade restrictions on imported wheat. He argued that limiting low-cost, high-quality wheat from countries with the right environment and soil conditions made no sense. Exporting goods that require skilled labor and machinery will provide more value to England. It could exchange for more wheat than it could produce on its own.

Why does trade protectionism fail in the long run? The principle of comparative advantage explains why. Politicians are constantly under pressure from their local residents to raise tariffs to defend employment from foreign competition. However, this is just a band-aid solution. It affects the country's competitiveness in the long run. It enables the country to squander money on failing industries. Consumers are often forced to pay higher rates for domestic products.

David Ricardo began his career as a successful stockbroker, earning more than $100 million in today's money. He became an economist after reading Adam Smith's "The Wealth of Nations." In England in 1809, he pointed out, large rises in the money supply caused inflation. Monetarism is the name given to this ideology.

He was also the one who came up with the concept of decreasing marginal returns. One of the fundamental principles in microeconomics is this. It claims that production is a point where the increased performance is no longer worth the extra raw material input.

## How Does It Work?

The enormous landmass of America, which is bordered by two oceans, is one of the country's competitive advantages. It also has a lot of fresh water, arable land, and oil that is readily available. Businesses in the United States profit from low-cost natural resources as well as defense from a land invasion.

Most importantly, it has a diverse population that speaks the same language and follows the same national rules. The diverse population serves as a large testing ground for new products. It aided the US in becoming a world leader in consumer goods production.

In finance, aerospace, defense machinery, and technology, diversity has aided the United States in becoming a global leader. Silicon Valley has made a name for itself as a pioneer in creative thinking by harnessing the strength of diversity. The US economy's strength stems from the combination of these advantages.

In the knowledge-based global economy, investing in human resources is crucial to retaining a competitive advantage.

## Absolute Advantage vs. Comparative Advantage

Anything a nation does more effectively than other countries is referred to as absolute advantage. Agriculture, diesel, and petrochemicals are all advantageous for countries with plenty of farmland, fresh water, and oil reserves.

A country's total advantage in one sector does not guarantee that it will be its competitive advantage in another. That is contingent on the trading opportunity costs. Let's say its next-door neighbor has no oil but plenty of farmland and clean water. In return for oil, the neighbor is willing to trade a lot of food. In terms of crude, the first nation now has a comparative advantage. Trading for oil allows it to obtain more food from its neighbor than it will produce on its own.

## Comparative Advantage vs. Competitive Advantage: What's the Difference?

What a country, company, or person does to provide a better value to customers than its competitors is referred to as competitive advantage. Companies use three tactics to achieve a competitive edge. They may, for starters, be a low-cost provider. Second, they may be able to provide a better product or service. Third, they could concentrate on a single customer segment.

## How Does It Affect You?

What you do best when giving up the least is referred to as comparative advantage. If you're a great plumber and a great babysitter, for example, plumbing is your competitive advantage. This is due to the fact that you can earn more money as a plumber. You can hire a babysitter for an hour for less than the cost of an hour of plumbing work. Babysitting has a high opportunity cost. Any hour you spend babysitting is an hour you should have been earning money on a plumbing job.

Something you do more effectively than anyone else is considered an absolute advantage. You're better at both plumbing and babysitting than anyone else in the area. However, you have a distinct advantage in the field of plumbing. That's because you're just willing to give up low-paying babysitting work in order to follow your well-paying plumbing career. 1 Competitive advantage is what distinguishes you from your rivals in terms of market appeal. 10 For example, your plumbing and babysitting services are in high demand. But it's not only that you're better at them (absolute advantage). It's because you're less expensive.

## Final Thoughts

Individuals, businesses, and nations participate in trade to profit from their advantages. These advantages may be absolute, comparative, or competitive.

The definition of comparative advantage is used by most countries when deciding whether to import or export. This is what it says:

• One country may have a competitive or absolute advantage over another. However, it also tends to focus output on a good or service that it can produce more effectively than its trading partners.

• A country with a comparative advantage uses its capital, labor, and natural resources to produce goods with lower opportunity costs and higher profit margins.

• Protectionism from trade protects inefficient industries. It allows resources to be squandered on uncompetitive production. This runs counter to the concept of comparative advantage.

• This idea was created by David Ricardo, an 18th-century economist. He wished to abolish tariffs on wheat imports into the United Kingdom.

**What is second-order thinking, and how does it differ from first-order thinking?**

We remain encased in a safe haven that is easily accessible to us and directs a large portion of our decisions. Our thoughts and beliefs are formed by a combination of our environment and experiences. This box has a major impact on how we think and make decisions.

As a theoretical model, second order thought necessitates stepping outside of our comfort zone and thinking outside the box. It necessitates a consideration of the long-term consequences of our decision. It necessitates the following inquiries:

How can I make decisions that will have a positive impact in the future?

Is this decision only appealing because it has an immediate positive effect (first order consequence)?

What are the possible consequences of this decision and how will they affect you later?

How far can I look to see how each subsequent decision opens up new possibilities or limits what I can accomplish?

Second order thinking is a framework for making decisions that involves learning the second order implications of our decisions and assessing their effectiveness in the near future. It's difficult to think beyond the second level, but some people will learn to extend their thinking to the third and beyond by asking the same questions at each level.

In his book Principles, Ray Dalio explains this very well.

Many painfully bad decisions are the result of failing to consider second- and third-order effects, and it's particularly dangerous when the first inferior choice reinforces your own biases. Never take the first available option, no matter how appealing it appears to be, without first asking questions and conducting research.

## What is the difference between first and second order thinking?

Let's first define the distinction between first and second order thought before learning how to use second order thinking to tap into the unknown. It's important to distinguish between the two in order to make a deliberate attempt to move from first to second order thought.

**Within the box thinking is first order thinking.**

First-level reasoning seeks simple solutions based on our previous experiences and values. It emphasizes the immediate effects of our decisions while ignoring the long-term consequences. Our first-order mentality is at work as we pursue immediate gratification.

System1 thought, which is intuitive and fast, activates it (Source: Thinking Fast And Slow by Daniel Kahneman). When we need to make fast decisions without exerting effort, this way of thinking is extremely useful. This category encompasses a large portion of our everyday choices, such as what to wear to work, where to meet a friend for dinner, and the turns to take on the way to work.

Because of the conventional nature of first-order reasoning, we are limited to achieving the same outcomes as anyone else.

To summarise, first-order thinking is safe, superficial, reactionary, obvious, fast, simple, and traditional, with an emphasis on immediate effect.

Second-order thought entails thinking beyond the box.

Second-level reasoning is difficult because it goes beyond our existing views and perceptions. It takes a lot of time and effort to uncover the long-term consequences of our decisions.

Given the complexities and uncertainties of our choices, it necessitates deliberate and rational system2 thought.

Great thinkers distinguish themselves from the average by going beyond intuition and finding unconventional ideas using second order thought theory. They outperform others and achieve greater success.

Second-order thinking is difficult, fluid, unpredictable, and unorthodox, with a willingness to investigate possible future outcomes and maximize its benefits.

How to Improve Second Order Thinking: A Decision-Making Template

**Let's learn to assess the influence of first order effects by developing a template using these measures to improve second order thought skills:**

1. Make a list of the first option that comes to mind, along with its immediate benefits and drawbacks. This is how you think in the first place.

2. Then, to determine the 2nd, 3rd, and nth level implications, ask, "What will be the potential consequences of this decision?" Make a list of the positives and negatives for each decision and stage.

3. To learn from your questions, keep asking yourself more and more questions.

What are the risks that this decision entails for me?

What effect will my decision have on others?

What do other people think of my decision?

Why do I believe my decision is correct?

Is it possible to use Occam's razor to find simpler solutions?

4. Choose the option with the most positive second and third order consequences, even if the first isn't (short term pain in favor of long term gain).

5. Recognize and implement feedback loops. It may not help you with your current decision right now, but it will help you make better decisions in the future.

You will see the positive results of your efforts compound over time once you adopt a second order thinking mental model and begin applying its template in your decision-making process.

Howard Marks, a well-known American investor and author, discusses first- and second-order thinking.

The workload difference between first- and second-level thinking is enormous, and the number of people capable of the latter is insignificant in comparison to the former. First-level thinkers seek simple formulas and straightforward solutions. Second-level thinkers understand that investing success is the polar opposite of simple.

## Framework for Reducing Regret

In life, you must occasionally make difficult choices. Perhaps you must choose between quitting your job, starting your own business, ending a relationship, or relocating to another country. These are the kinds of big decisions you have to make entirely on your own. Although having the support of your surroundings is beneficial, you are still on your own at the end of the day. You are the one who must decide whether or not to move.

Just before he quit his job and founded Amazon, Jeff Bezos was in the same situation. He had a well-paid Wall Street job, a steady career, a good boss, and a healthy lifestyle. But he had this crazy idea of starting his own company and selling books online. His wife backed him up completely, and the people around him thought it was a great idea. He needed to make a choice.

He looked for theories and recommendations on how to make such major decisions because it was a difficult decision. Because he couldn't find any good advice on the subject, he devised a framework to assist him in making the best decision possible. Regret Minimization Framework was his nerdy name for it.

The Regret Minimization Framework is based on a simple concept. Now imagine yourself at the age of 80. You want to have as few regrets as possible when you look back on your life. Things become a lot clearer when you project yourself to the age of 80 and consider your potential regrets. It also aids in the removal of some present-day ambiguity caused by alternative paths. It makes it easier for you to make the best decision possible.

All the things you know you'll regret if you don't at least try to achieve in your life should be at the very top of your life vision list. We all have a few things on our bucket lists, whether it's a specific country to visit, a specific mountain to climb, a specific thing to create, a specific adventure to go on with other people, or something else entirely. Don't let fear or compromises keep you from experiencing things you'll come to regret later. When a chance arises, use the Regret Minimization Framework to assist you in making the best decision possible.

But beware: don't be fooled by pretty motivational stories like this. You don't want to use the Regret Minimization Framework to justify a bad decision. Everyday small decisions (what you eat every day, how you spend your money, and so on) and major big decisions (who you marry, where you work, and so on) play a role in either your success or failure in life. So make a list of your potential regrets, but keep in mind your current level of expertise, the appropriate timing, environmental factors, and other factors.

## What Is Parkinson's Law and How Does It Work?

According to Parkinson's Law of Time, "work expands to fill the time available for completion."

Whether you're working on a creative project, a school paper, or a task for your 9-5 job, the amount of time you have will determine how long it takes you to complete it.

Cyril Northcote Parkinson created the law in 1955 as part of an essay for The Economist. It is a well-known fact that work expands to fill the time allotted for its completion.

An elderly lady of leisure, for example, could spend the entire day writing and mailing a postcard to her niece in Bognor Regis. An hour will be spent looking for the postcard, another hour will be spent looking for spectacles, a half-hour will be spent looking for the address, an hour and a quarter will be spent composing, and twenty minutes will be spent deciding whether or not to take an umbrella to the pillar-box across the street.

After a day of doubt, anxiety, and toil, the total effort that would take a busy man three minutes all told may leave another person prostrate.

The longer you have to complete a task, the longer it will take you to complete it.

John Murray, another researcher, applied Parkinson's Law to government cabinets. Smaller teams, he discovered, were often the most efficient. There was more room for arbitrary debate as groups grew larger, and more time was wasted. "Officials make work for each other," writes Parkinson in his essay.

You waste more time the more time you have.

The more time you have to complete a project, the longer it will take you. You'll procrastinate, "research," look into side issues and opportunities, debate with yourself arbitrarily, and basically do anything but what you're supposed to be doing.

Procrastination has a lot of power. But there is reason to be optimistic. Read on for a few easy ways to boost your productivity and time management.

Continually. Everything is in place. There are deadlines to meet.

The stress of a looming deadline is the ultimate motivator. When you're in a rush to finish something, your mind takes over and make it happen.

That's the kind of deadline you should set for yourself: one that feels nearly impossible to meet.

Setting a hard deadline works because we have a hard time estimating how long something will take. You'll have a much better idea once you get started.

As a result, make aggressive deadlines. Then, as you go along, revise them.

With an aggressive deadline, do only the most important work.

According to Parkinson's Law, work expands to fill the time available.

The Pareto Principle (also known as the 80/20 rule) states that 20% of all causes or possible factors account for 80% of the outcomes in any given event.

So, what if you set aggressive deadlines for only the most important inputs?

In his book The 4 Hour Workweek, Tim Ferriss calls this powerful combination. This is a very strange phenomenon, writes Ferriss.

**There are two inversions of each other in terms of synergistic approaches to increasing productivity:**

1. To reduce work time, limit tasks to the most significant (80/20).

2. Reduce job time and focus on the most critical things (Parkinson's Law).

The best option is to combine the two: Determine the few crucial activities that have the greatest impact on income and schedule them with *extremely short* and transparent deadlines.

This simple passage has completely transformed the way I spend my time.

You'll be amazed by how much progress you can make on your major goals in just a short period of time if you start doing this. You'll also begin to take Peter Thiel's challenge of completing the 10-year plan in six months seriously.

The Effect of Parkinson's Law on Productivity

Parkinson's Principle has the greatest effect on procrastination. When you ignore too much time for a mission, you are wasting valuable time that could be used elsewhere.

Many individuals, even though they aren't aware of it, are procrastinators. Have you ever waited until the last minute to complete a mission under the guise of "doing well under pressure"? Then you've got procrastination. This occurs when you think you have more than enough time to complete a task. And if an activity is expected to take one hour but you give it three, it will last that long.

To fill the allotted time, the job will become more complicated, according to Parkinson's Law. The extra time you put in isn't always reflected in the final product. Before they get around to doing the job, the majority of people will panic, tense, and stress about it.

When it comes to running a company, employee efficiency is crucial. You want workers who can complete their tasks in the most productive manner possible. Spending just as much time on checklists as is required increases efficiency.

## How to Use Your Time More Effectively

So, you've heard about Parkinson's Law. How are you going to apply that lesson to change your habits?

In order to avoid wasting time, effective time management is needed. Start by shortening deadlines. When making a to-do list or planning a project, make sure you just set aside enough time. Remove the possibility of procrastination. Short deadlines compel employees to concentrate on the basics. To ensure that the job is completed, you will make the most of the available time. Bear in mind, however, that deadlines should be fair. Make a detailed assessment of the mission so that you can allocate sufficient time to it

## How do you do more in less time?

An easy way to combat Parkinson's Law is to change our mentality and stop thinking that in order to complete a mission, we must use up all of the time allocated.

When it comes to maximizing your time, productivity and time-management methodologies and strategies can be extremely beneficial.

## Techniques for Productivity and Time Management

Each job is assigned a particular block of time using the time-blocking technique.

The 2-Minute Rule in GTD (Getting Things Done)

The GTD (Getting Things Done) two-minute rule states that any job that can be accomplished in less than two minutes should be completed right away rather than being planned or added to a to-do list.

The Pareto principle is a set of rules.

The Pareto principle, also known as the 80/20 law, states that only 20% of a task's effort yields 80% of the outcome. That is to say, the bulk of the work has a minor effect on the end product.

You can use a Pareto map to assist you.

Technique of the Pomodoro

The Pomodoro Strategy consists of 25-minute concentrated work sprints separated by a 5-minute break to help maintain concentration and minimize mental exhaustion.

## Quick intervals of time

Sessions of concentrated work – with regular short breaks

Reducing time waste and increasing efficiency

When it comes to reducing time waste and increasing productivity, effective resource planning is essential. For starters, hire the right people for the right jobs. Task management is essential because workers with the appropriate skills for the assigned tasks know where to begin. They aren't going to waste time figuring out how to approach a task. Make a list of the other resources you'll need for the job. If a project necessitates the purchase of new equipment, do so ahead of time. Members of the team will not have to waste time looking for what they require.

Accountability is key if you are to meet tight deadlines. A degree of accountability helps a great deal, whether a worker is alone or part of a team. If a project encounters an issue, there should be a practical and effective way to deal with it. Know who to hold responsible when the deliverables are not met.

# Chapter 3 the Role of mental Models?

## Building Self-Confidence

Putting You in a Position to Succeed!

Everyone admires a self-confident person. We might even be envious of them! Self-assured people appear to be at ease with themselves and their work. They invite others to trust them and instill confidence in them. These are all appealing qualities.

It's not always easy to believe in yourself, especially if you're naturally critical of yourself or if others criticize you. However, there are steps you can take to boost and maintain your self-esteem.

## What Is Self-Confidence, and Why Do I Need It?

Self-confidence is knowing that you can trust your own judgment and abilities, and that you value and feel worthy of yourself, despite any flaws or what others may think of you.

Self-efficacy and self-esteem are often confused with self-confidence, but they are not the same thing.

When we see ourselves (and others like us) mastering skills and achieving goals, we gain a sense of self-efficacy. This gives us hope that we can succeed if we learn and work hard in a specific area. This kind of self-assurance motivates people to take on difficult tasks and persevere in the face of setbacks.

Self-esteem refers to the belief that we can deal with whatever life throws at us and that we have the right to be happy.

Often, part of our self-esteem stems from the belief that those around us agree with us. We may or may not be capable to control this, and if we are subjected to a lot of criticism or disapproval from others, our self-esteem may suffer unless we have additional help.

**Behavior and Confidence**

Consider the examples in the table below, which contrast optimistic behavior with behavior associated with a lack of self-confidence. Whatever feelings or behaviors do you see in yourself and others around you?

Behaviors Associated With Low Self-Confidence Confident Behaviors Associated With Low Self-Confidence

Even if some ridicule or blame you for doing what you think is right.

Governing your actions based on the opinions of others.

Willingness to take chances and go the extra mile in order to produce better results.

Avoiding risk, staying in your comfort zone, and fearing failure.

Accepting responsibility for the errors and learning from them.

Working tirelessly to conceal errors in the hopes of resolving the issue before anyone sees.

You're waiting for people to compliment you on your achievements.

Extolling your own values to as many people as you can.

Accepting compliments with grace. "Thank you; I put a lot of effort into that prospectus. I'm glad you appreciate my efforts." Offhandedly dismissing compliments. "Oh, the prospectus was nothing; anyone could have done it."

Low self-confidence, as these examples demonstrate, can be self-destructive and manifest itself as negativity.

People who are self-assured are usually more upbeat; they admire themselves and believe in their own judgment. They do, however, accept and learn from their shortcomings and mistakes.

## Why Is Self-Belief Important?

While self-confidence is important in almost every aspect of our lives, many people struggle to find it. Unfortunately, this may become a vicious cycle: people who lack self-confidence are less likely to gain the success that would boost their self-esteem.

You may not want to support a project pitched by someone who is clearly anxious, fumbling, or continually apologizing, for example. On the other hand, someone who talks plainly, holds their head high, confidently answers questions, and readily admits when they don't know anything can convince you.

Confident people instill trust in those around them, like their audience, coworkers, managers, clients, and friends. And one of the most important ways to succeed is to win the trust of others. We'll show you how to do it in the parts below.

## Suggestion:

Take our quick quiz to see how self-assured you are right now and to learn about unique strategies that can help you boost your trust.

## How to Make You Think You is More Confident

You may demonstrate self-assurance in a variety of ways, including your behavior, body language, and what you say and how you say it.

Self-confidence can be improved by projecting a positive picture to others. It isn't just a case of "faking it." Others are more likely to react positively if you project trust, and this positive reinforcement will make you believe in yourself.

Body Language is an essential aspect of communication.

Take a relaxed, open stance. Place your hands by your sides and sit or stand straight. Standing with your hands on your hips will send the message that you want to be in control. Make sure you don't slouch!

Keep your head straight and upright. Inclining too far forward or backward can make you appear violent. If you're giving a presentation, use open hand gestures.

With your palms turned slightly to your audience, spread your hands apart. This demonstrates a desire to engage and exchange ideas. Maintain a near relationship between your upper arms and your body.

## Face-to-Face Interaction

When meeting a customer, addressing a meeting or making a presentation, people with low self-confidence often struggle to make a successful first impression. You may be shy or self-conscious, but there are steps you can take right now to appear more confident.

Maintaining eye contact while speaking is critical for engaging with people. This demonstrates that you're paying attention to what they're saying and that you're participating in the discussion. When it comes to body language and communication, however, keep in mind some cultural considerations.

While the conversation is going on, don't fidget or look away, as this will make you seem distracted or nervous.

If shaking hands is the standard greeting at your place of business, be firm. But don't be too firm, and don't be too forthright. Reaching for the other person's wrist or arm with your free hand is frequently interpreted as a sign of superiority, and it's not a good idea for a first date. Make sure the experience isn't uncomfortable – or worse, painful!

**Defeating Short-Term Self-Confidence Obstacles**

Even the most outwardly self-assured individual may have doubts about their abilities. You can, for example, have a knack for coming up with brilliant ideas or solutions but fail to be heard in meetings. Alternatively, you could be forced to work from home for an extended period of time and feel lost or alone without the company of your coworkers.

To deal with short-term trust drops, try to figure out what's causing the problem.

If you're having trouble keeping your faith because of stuff you think you can't do, it's time to brush up on your skills. To define your strengths and weaknesses, conduct a Personal SWOT Analysis. Then make an action plan to improve the areas where you are weak.

Other people's attitudes or behavior can exacerbate your loss of trust. If you're being insulted or experiencing microaggressions at work, or if you believe people are making inaccurate assumptions about you, you should speak up.

You may use the Situation-Behavior-Impact Feedback Tool to let the person in charge know that their actions are negative. If that doesn't work, ask your line manager for assistance. Talk with HR if they're a part of the issue. Bullying in the workplace should not be tolerated.

To develop a sense that you have rights and needs as an individual, practice assertiveness, and make sure that others understand and respect your personal boundaries. This will aid in the development of psychological safety, which is essential for self-confidence.

People with low self-esteem often believe that they are unworthy of happiness and that they deserve to be handled badly. Although the sensation may be accurate, the conviction is not!

## How Do You Gain and Maintain Self-Confidence?

Short-term action can help with immediate or acute self-esteem problems, but longer-term confidence building requires more fundamental action. This can include making lifestyle changes as well as making solid long-term plans.

## Making Self-Assured Habits

Aim to cultivate positive habits (and break bad ones!) in order to develop a strong sense of self-esteem and the trust that comes with it.

Take care of your physical and mental well-being; daily exercise will help with both. Check to see if you're having enough sleep and eating well. Not doing so will make you feel better for yourself and make you feel bad about yourself.

Working on your professional branding will also boost your self-esteem. If you can project an optimistic picture of your true self, you'll begin to obtain the positive feedback that is so crucial to your self-esteem.

## Examining Previous Achievements

When you can say, "I can do this, and here's the evidence," you can boost your self-esteem. You'll have found stuff you're fantastic at based on your previous successes as part of your Personal SWOT Analysis.

In a "achievement log," write down the ten things you're most proud of. Perhaps you excelled on a difficult test or exam, contributed significantly to a crucial team or mission, or did something kind that made a meaningful difference in someone else's life.

Examine your accomplishments and use them to reinforce optimistic affirmations about your abilities. If you tend to undermine your own self-confidence with negative self-talk, these affirmations may be especially effective.

## Setting Confidence-Building Objectives

Setting and achieving goals is an important aspect of self-confidence growth. Goal setting is the practice of setting goals for yourself and measuring how well you achieve them.

Your Own SWOT Analysis will help you set goals. Set targets that take advantage of your strengths, minimize your weaknesses, maximize your resources, and minimize the challenges you face.

Determine the first move for each of the big goals you want to accomplish after you've defined them. Make sure it's a minor move that shouldn't take more than an hour to complete.

If you start to have questions when you're setting goals, write them down and challenge them calmly and rationally. It's better if they seem less serious when questioned. However, if they are focused on real threats, make sure you set additional targets to address them.

Big targets become much more attainable when they are broken down into smaller steps like this. It also lets you keep track of your success and look back on how far you've come.

## What Are Problem-Solving Skills and How Do You Develop Them?

Problem-solving abilities assist you in efficiently and effectively resolving problems. It's one of the most important qualities that employers look for in job candidates, as workers with these abilities are more self-sufficient. Problem-solving abilities necessitate rapidly finding the root problem and putting a solution in place.

Problem-solving is a soft skill (a personal strength), not a hard skill that can be mastered through education or training. By familiarizing yourself with common problems in your field and learning from more seasoned employees, you will develop your problem-solving abilities.

## Problem-Solving Techniques in Action

Identifying the problem is the first step in problem-solving. A instructor, for example, would need to find out how to increase a student's writing proficiency test score. To do so, the instructor will go over the writing tests and search for places where they can develop. Students may be able to create simple sentences, but they struggle to write paragraphs and organize those paragraphs into an essay.

## 1. Examine the Factors That Contribute

To solve a problem, you must first determine the source of the issue. This necessitates gathering and analyzing data, identifying potential contributing factors, and determining what needs to be done in order to reach a resolution.

You'll need skills like: • data collection • data analysis • fact-finding • historical analysis to accomplish this.

## 2. Come up with interventions

After you've figured out what's causing the problem, come up with some ideas. Since two (or more) minds are sometimes stronger than one, this often necessitates teamwork. A single approach is not the obvious solution to a complicated problem; creating a list of options allows you cover all of your bases and reduces the chance of being exposed if the first strategy fails.

This necessitates the use of skills such as brainstorming and creative thinking.

Prediction, forecasting, project design, and project preparation are all things that come to mind when it comes to project design and planning.

## 3. Assessing Alternatives

Delegated teams can do evaluations of best options, team leads, or forwarded to organizational decision-makers, depending on the nature of the issue and the chain of command. Whoever makes the decision must consider the potential costs, resources needed, and obstacles to an effective solution implementation.

This necessitates a variety of abilities, including: • analysis • discussion • corroboration • teamwork • test creation • mediation • prioritization

## 4. Put the Plan into Action

After deciding on a course of action, it must be enforced with metrics that can easily and reliably assess if it is working. Notifying employees of improvements in standard operating procedures is often part of the plan implementation process.

This necessitates the creation of skills such as: • project management • project delivery • collaboration • time management • benchmark development

## 5. Evaluate the solution's efficacy

The best problem-solvers have processes in place to determine whether and how effectively a solution is working after it is implemented. This way, they'll know as soon as possible if the problem has been resolved or whether they'll need to adjust their answer to it in the middle of the process.

• Communication is needed.

• Analyzing data

• Customer input • Surveys • Follow-up • Troubleshooting

**Another way to demonstrate your problem-solving abilities in a cover letter is to:**

### Emphasizing Problem-Solving Capabilities

Put them front and center on your resume, cover letter, and in interviews, as this is an ability that most employers value.

If you're unsure what to include, think back to previous positions for examples of obstacles you've faced and issues you've overcome, whether in academia, the workplace, or as a volunteer. In your cover letter, provide specific examples, and in your resume, use bullet points to explain how you solved a problem.

Prepare to explain situations you've faced in previous positions, the methods you used to solve problems, the skills you used, and the outcomes of your decisions during interviews. Potential employers are interested in hearing a coherent story about how you've applied problem-solving skills.

Interviewers can ask you to solve hypothetical problems. Base your responses on the five measures and, if possible, related problems you've solved. Here are several pointers on how to respond to problem-solving interview questions, along with examples of the best responses.

## Making a Decision

### Decision-Making That Works

Both on a personal or organizational basis, decisions must be able to be executed. As a result, you must be personally committed to the decision and be willing to convince others of its merits.

As a result, an efficient decision-making process must ensure that you are capable of doing so.

### What can obstruct good decision-making?

There are a slew of problems that can stymie good decision-making. There are some of them:

### 1. Insufficient information

It can seem like you're making a decision without any justification if you don't have enough details.

Even if you're on a tight deadline, take some time to collect the information you'll need to make an informed decision. Prioritize your information gathering if possible, by determining which information is most valuable to you.

## 2. Excessive Information

The polar opposite problem, but surprisingly common one: getting so much opposing information that it is difficult to see "the forest for the trees."

This is known as analysis paralysis, and it's also a strategy for delaying organizational decision-making by having those involved demand ever more information before making a decision.

This issue is often solved by bringing everyone together to determine what information is really relevant and why and establishing a specific timeframe for decision-making that includes a stage for collecting information.

## 3. There Are So Many People

It's difficult to make decisions by committee. Everyone has their own perspectives and beliefs. While it's hard to comprehend these points of view and why and how they matter, it might be necessary for one person to take responsibility for making a decision. Any choice is sometimes preferable to none.

## 4. Conflicts of Interest

The weight of vested interests often causes decision-making processes to fail. These vested interests are rarely voiced openly, but they can be a major roadblock. It may be difficult to recognize them and then discuss them since they are not overtly articulated, but it is often possible to explore them with someone outside the process who is in a similar role.

It may also be beneficial to discuss the rational/intuitive aspects with all stakeholders, usually with the assistance of an external facilitator.

Emotional Attachments are number five.

People often love the status quo. Decisions always include the possibility of transition, which many people dread.

### 6. There Isn't Any Emotional Attachment

It can be difficult to make a decision when you don't really care one way or the other. A systematic decision-making process will also aid in this situation by recognizing the very real pros and cons of specific behavior that you might not have considered before.

**A formal decision-making process can help solve many of these problems. This will assist in:**

• Break down more difficult decisions into smaller steps; • examine how decisions are made; and • schedule decision-making to meet deadlines.

Several different decision-making strategies developed, ranging from basic rules of thumb to highly complex procedures. The procedure used is determined by the complexity of the decision to be made and the quality of the decision to be made.

# Chapter 4 Mental Models for Critical Thinking and how the Most Successful People Think Differently?

It's fascinating to consider why some people are more effective than others, particularly if you're setting high goals for yourself. What would it take for people like Richard Branson, Elon Musk, and Bill Gates to continue to succeed and achieve the highest levels of success?

Of necessity, the solutions are complicated. But that doesn't rule out the possibility of learning them. Of these successful people has a collection of smart mindsets that all of us can adopt, which will benefit us regardless of our level of success.

**The following are seven of the best examples:**

**1. Successful people are unconcerned with failure.**

They see failure as an opportunity to start all over again, except this time more wisely. They understand that it isn't a life-changing occurrence, and they don't consider it a concern until it becomes a habit. They win as if it's second nature to them, and they lose as if they relish the challenge.

## 2. People who are successful embrace who they are and what they stand for.

You won't be able to step forward if you keep putting yourself down. According to successful people, self-acceptance–refusing to have an adversarial relationship with yourself–is the smartest attitude you may have.

## 3. People who are successful set targets and work hard to achieve them.

Having a dream is wonderful, but having a dream and goals is even better, because goals are the means by which dreams can be realized. The most effective people are still setting and achieving targets in order to have a positive impact. Goals make the invisible visible; they allow you to organize your thought so that you're still searching for something you can do to get closer to your objectives. Goals motivate you to ask yourself every day, "What am I doing today that will get me closer to where I want to be and what I want to achieve?" Not only do successful people set targets, but they also set them high. They don't stop until they've arrived at their destination.

## 4. Successful people don't take chances with their lives.

Rather than passively hoping for the best, they take charge of the situation and make it happen. You still have the option of controlling or allowing your mind to rule you. Refusing to let something happen by chance demonstrates inner power, determination, and a strong will. When you decide to take care of what you can control and let go of the rest, amazing things happen.

## 5. Successful people don't let challenges get in the way of their goals.

If you have a pessimistic attitude, challenges will develop in intensity and drag you down continuously, taking you on thinking detours into some poor neighborhoods. On the other hand, problems can be seen as an opportunity to be imaginative and come up with novel ideas if you have a positive attitude. The main issue is that we think of issues as such. Successful people understand that focusing on challenges leads to more problems, while focusing on possibilities leads to more opportunities.

## 6. Decisiveness is a trait of successful people.

The most effective people are able to make quick decisions. They don't second-guess themselves or waffle.

They gather the information they need, then clear their heads and choose the best choice based on their knowledge. They learn from it if it turns out to be incorrect. They will not, however, be accused of failing to make a decision.

## 7. People who are successful are still learning.

Borrow the shoshin, or learner's mind, mentality from Zen Buddhism if you want to go far. That you don't claim to know everything but are open to learning, growth, and development, with an open, enthusiastic, and bias-free mind. We can all learn from experience, but you must be teachable to take advantage of it.

## Ways to Improve Your Decision-Making Skills in an Unusual Way

## 1. Incorporate arts and entertainment into the daily routine.

This could range from weekly salsa lessons to including opera performances in your monthly calendar. Try learning to play the guitar for an hour three days a week, or try painting scenes from your favorite movie with gouache. While it may seem time-consuming, investing time in arts and culture can pay off in the form of improved focus and an improvement in your overall mood, both of which are beneficial when making decisions. If you try something special, something you've never done before, like sculpture modeling or learning to play the harp, you'll get the most powerful decision-making benefits.

## 2. Develop your coding or language skills

Study on something more technical to engage a particular part of your brain. You could work on improving your writing skills or learning a new language. Otherwise, immerse yourself in programming or learn to use some useful tools. This strategy kills two birds with one stone; devoting free time to learning IT or developing your foreign language skills would almost certainly result in you adding extra value to your resume.

## 3. Interact with people of various ages.

Attempt to broaden the age spectrum of those in your immediate vicinity. Maintain contact with people who are older than you as well as those who are far younger. Contact with the first group can help you become more mindful and successful at preparing for the future, while contact with the second group can help you remember your previous dreams, accomplishments, and failures. Although previous victories will instill optimism and trust, errors will ensure that you do not step on the same rake twice.

**Ways to Make More Informed Life Choices**

Making better choices is one of the most valuable life skills you can teach yourself. Every one of us has the ability to make decisions. If we know it or not, we are faced with hundreds of decisions every day. All of your everyday behaviorsand actions are the product of a choice you make. If you want to live a happier life, it is up to you to make wise choices so that you do not regret anything later. Your future is shaped by the actions you take every second of the day. The time is ticking... Would you like to learn how to make better decisions and live a life without regrets? Then stick to these five pointers!

**1. Make a list of your objectives.**

The first step in making better life decisions is to figure out what your true objectives are. Make a list of things you want to do in your life before you die. This may include marriage, earning a college diploma, maintaining a healthy lifestyle, or landing a well-paying career. Once you've done your list, make a list of items you can do to help you achieve your objectives. If you want to get a better paying career, you should consider going to college. If you want to marry but have no experience with relationships, you should focus on improving your situation. Alternatively, if you want to stay in shape, make sure you stick to normal exercise routines. Identifying your aspirations and focusing more of your time and resources on them is the first step toward making smarter life decisions, whatever it is that you want out of life.

## 2. Examine the Advantages and Disadvantages

Now that you know exactly what you want out of life and have a strategy in place to achieve your objectives, you must weigh the benefits and drawbacks of each of your everyday activities. Consider if what you're doing right now, every day, is sufficient to achieve your objectives. Consider if you're doing too much and should cut back, or if you're doing too little and should increase your efforts.

## 3. Acknowledge and Learn From Your Mistakes

You'll have to learn from your own mistakes if you want to make better choices in life. Everyone has made a mistake at some point in their lives, no matter how large or small. Nobody is without flaws. Rather than berating yourself for past errors, you should take the opportunity to learn from them. It's better to learn from your mistakes now rather than repeating them later! You never know when you'll face a similar challenge again, so don't underestimate the value of learning from your mistakes.

## 4. Learn from the mistakes of others

You should not only learn from your own mistakes, but you should also look at other people's mistakes and learn from what they've done wrong. If you just concentrate on your own mistakes, you will be unable to learn how to prevent the mistakes that others have made and that you will make in the future. You should speak with people who are older than you and find out what they regret or did wrong in their lives so that you can be more informed to escape the same fate.

## 5. Trust Your Gut Feelings

Pay attention to your gut instincts or the voice inside your brain. If you believe what you're doing is right, don't hesitate to challenge yourself or others; just keep doing what you're doing. Avoid doing what you're doing if you think it's wrong or has a negative impact on your life. Excessive substance use, video game play, walking home at night, and unhealthy eating are all items you can stop if you want to live a life without regrets. Other things you should be doing include talking to your crush, going the extra mile at school or work, and supporting others.

And keep in mind that making better life decisions isn't just about understanding what's right or wrong; it's also about doing what's right. The fewer things you do wrong in life, the fewer regrets you will have. And it's not just about what you do in life; it's also about what you don't do. In life, doing nothing is just as bad as doing things incorrectly.

# Chapter 5 Mental Models for Personal Life

## How to Change Your Mind and Change Your Life in Practical Ways

### Mindset Work's Importance

Spending time on attitude work is extremely important. We begin to understand ourselves during this period, and as a result of that understanding, we become more compassionate and patient with ourselves.

Our community and culture thrive on the busyness that life brings into our lives, even at the dinner table. As a result of relying on "band-aid" solutions and easy fixes to get us through difficult times in our lives, there are certainly unintended consequences. Those strategies never last, and it takes time and effort to slow down, ground ourselves, and refocus our attention.

Changing your mindset not only allows you to be more confident, but it also allows your mind to evolve and develop. It's about examining all that hasn't evolved for you so far and being open to new possibilities.

## How to Alter Your Thought Process and Change Your Life

## Here are 11 ideas to help you change your mind:

### 1. Be on time.

You don't want to go to the gym? Regardless, go. After making a promise to practice every day, you don't feel like playing the piano? Do it and have fun with it.

Showing up and committing pays off handsomely. It boosts your self-esteem, and as a result, your attitude shifts.

Of course, turning up isn't always enjoyable, but completing the smaller goals on your list helps you to focus on the larger goals that might seem insurmountable.

### 2. Locate an Anchor

We all need an anchor, or something in which to place our faith when our thoughts become erratic. Keep on to what you have, whether you are religious, have a spiritual bond with a higher power, or have someone that grounds you.

When my father first told me about the Law of Attraction when I was 17, I thought it was a joke and never gave it much thought. After ten years, the Law of Attraction has been so ingrained in my everyday routine that it has become the foundation of my belief system. The anchor is also what motivates me to be a better person. It's a ray of hope when I've persuaded myself that there is no such thing as light.

An anchor aims to keep you grounded when your mind and/or external influences are weighing you down. When something else seems to be going wrong, it's about having confidence and trust in that one thing or force. If you want to start changing your attitude, this is one of the most important things you'll need.

### 3. Find out why.

That's what there is to it. You must delve further into what is triggering a reaction in order to improve your mindset.

•Why does it annoy me that someone else took the parking spot where I was supposed to be?

• Why do I get nervous when I eat alone in a restaurant?

• What makes me happy when I buy a new outfit?

We ask "why" to a lot of things outside of ourselves, but we rarely ask it of ourselves. It's also a way to get to know yourself in the same way that you might get to know a friend.

When we begin to address these questions, we learn that happiness, depression, remorse, and joy are more about knowing our own beliefs than external influences.

When you do ask these "whys," have a talk with yourself and focus on your responses.

For example, I'm annoyed at this person for taking my parking spot because I'm busy and have a long list of errands to run. I don't have time to search for a new role.

4. Take a Risk and Leave Your Comfort Zone

We all have a comfort zone, as previously said. We, like turtles, feel protected and secure within our shells, but in order to change your mind, you must be willing to leave the shell, no matter how comfortable it feels.

If we allow ourselves to be open to the possibilities of change, our attitude will begin to shift. Getting out of your comfort zone is one of the most difficult things you can do, but it all comes down to trust.

Some of my closest friendships have developed as a result of the five seconds I took to venture out of my comfort zone, introduce myself, and strike up a conversation.

Every day, try to learn something different, even if it makes you nervous at first.

## 5. Take a different perspective on things

I once inquired about a friend's definition of self-love. "Self-love means being a parent to yourself," she replied.

That response surprised me, but it set my mind spinning as I considered other meanings of what self-love could mean to others and myself.

Changing your mindset often entails being open to new ideas, particularly if they contradict your own. The more attitude training you do, the more you'll notice that you're approaching new opinions and concepts from a more grounded and relaxing spot. Things that used to make you defensive will gradually turn into a source of interest.

## 6. Take it easy.

Here's the deal: You commute to work on the same road and leave your house at the same time. You stop by your local coffee shop to order your everyday brew as you exit the highway, then you're out the door and on your way to the office.

Have you ever noticed the color of the corner building right before you exit the highway during your everyday routine? Have you ever considered whether your barista is right-handed or left-handed?

Probably not, since we seem to live our lives on autopilot the majority of the time.

Slowing down is one way to improve your attitude. Slowing down allows you to tune in to the same beat and sounds as the world around you. You start to notice what connects with you and what doesn't. You begin to be more aware of your surroundings.

You must be present in the life you are actually living if you want to change it. Being present allows you to transition into a grateful mind.

## How to Achieve Your Life Objectives

If you're having trouble realizing your dreams, these ten suggestions will help. Here's how to set and accomplish objectives.

## 1 Make a list of goals that inspire you.

Set personal goals for yourself that will motivate you to achieve new heights. Don't go along with the crowd and try to emulate your friends' ambitions; instead, do something you're passionate about and that truly interests you. This will help you develop a sense of mission, encouraging you to stop thinking and start doing.

## 2 Be proactive in your approach.

Life goals are those things you hope to achieve "one day," but never now. If you want to make something happen, you need to change your approach. Stop scrolling through social media, wishing you had that career, that lifestyle, that social life, and instead get out there and do something about it.

## 3 There Will Be No More Negativity

Earl Nightingale, an American writer, once said, "Our attitude toward life decides life's attitude toward us," and he was right. If you project negativity out into the universe, it will come back to bite you. You won't be able to do it if you tell yourself "you can't do this and you can't do that." Even if you're faking it, getting a "can do" mentality, as cliche as it might sound, can help you achieve your objectives. Whenever doubt creeps into your mind, swat it away and remind yourself that the glass is half full.

**4 Maintain a healthy balance.**

It's quick to get fixated on setting goals. You're addicted and will go to any length to achieve your goals. However, there is a chance of burnout if you do this. From the start, be honest about your goals. Drive is admirable, but keep in mind that you, like anyone else, need rest and recuperation.

Make a schedule for yourself and allot enough time per day or week to focus on your target. If you want to run a 10k race, for example, the first step should be to create a training schedule that includes the appropriate amount of training while avoiding fatigue. Do you need assistance? To get started, look at our list of challenges.

**5 Take It Apart**

Setting and achieving targets is difficult. There are no simple options or shortcuts, but that is part of what makes the experience so satisfying.

Break it down if you start to feel stressed. Not only in terms of time, but also in terms of action points. Outlining what you want to achieve, when you want to achieve it, and how you intend to achieve it will make your goals sound far more attainable.

## 6 Accept Failure

Setting goals is rarely easy. You'll run into roadblocks that make you wonder why you tried in the first place, but that's part of the process, and the sooner you embrace it, the better. Rather than allowing failure to defeat you, accept that it has occurred and learn from it. Make a list of what worked and what didn't, and then move on. You'll become a better goal-setter as a result of it.

## 7 Please inform all.

The first rule in goal-setting is to speak about it. Tell someone who would listen about your dreams and how you want to carry them out. The added pressure will push you to follow through with your thoughts. Furthermore, it offers networking opportunities. Developing long-term market objectives? The more people you talk to, the more likely you are to meet people with whom you can work and achieve your goals.

## 8 Seek assistance

Don't go it alone. There's only so far a project can go until it necessitates a change of perspective. This could be anything; maybe you're training for a half marathon and can't seem to get your PB under the enviable 2 hour mark no matter how hard you try.

**9 Keep an eye on your progress**

Seeing how far you've come can be a big motivator to get to the finish line. If your weight loss progress has come to a halt and you're tempted to revert to old (bad) habits, remind yourself of how far you've come so far.

Take videos, keep a journal, or even vlog your goal-setting trip. Keeping track of your good and bad weeks will also help you identify your flaws and figure out how to overcome them.

10 Create a mental image of the final product.

You'll be tempted to stray if you lose sight of the end goal. Visualizing the transformation you want to see is one of the most effective ways to stay motivated. Make this mental picture of yourself - the "you" in X number of weeks - so that you will not be discouraged and will bounce back better than ever if you have a loss.

The Advantages of Having an Open Mind

## What Does Being Open-Minded Imply?

**Open-mindedness can be divided into many categories:**

• The word "open-minded" is sometimes used as a synonym for "non-prejudiced" or "tolerant" in daily conversation.

• From a psychological perspective, the word refers to people's willingness to accept alternative viewpoints or pursue new experiences.

Asking questions and being proactive in the search for evidence that contradicts your convictions are examples of open-mindedness.

It also includes the conviction that other people should be able to share their opinions and points, even though you don't agree with them.

Closed-mindedness or dogmatism are the polar opposites of open-mindedness. Closed-minded people are generally only able to hear their own points of view and are not open to new ideas.

Even if you consider yourself to be a reasonably open-minded individual, there are likely some subjects on whom you take a much harder stance: for example, personal experiences or social issues. It's cool to have convictions, but that doesn't mean you can't keep an open mind. Being open-minded entails understanding different points of view and attempting to empathize with others, even though you disagree with them.

Open-mindedness, of course, has its limits. It doesn't mean you have to agree with every viewpoint. However, putting forward the effort to comprehend the reasons that could have contributed to those beliefs will aid in the development of strategies for persuading people to change their minds.

## Open-Minded People's Characteristics

• They want to know what other people think.

• They are open to having their theories questioned.

• They are not upset when they are wrong. • They have empathy for others. • They consider what other people are thinking. • They are humble in their own experience and skills. • They want to hear what other people have to tell. • They believe others have the right to express their views and opinions.

Being more open-minded has a number of practical and powerful advantages. You will benefit from open-mindedness in the following ways:

• Gain knowledge. Challenging your own views and considering new ideas will provide you with new perspectives on the world as well as new insights into yourself.

• Expand your horizons. Being receptive to new ideas can also lead to new experiences.

• Achieve professional growth. Maintaining an open mind will assist you in developing as a human. You gain new knowledge about the environment and the people in it.

•Develop mental fortitude. Keeping an open mind to new ideas and experiences will help you develop into a more powerful and vibrant person. Your awareness and experiences continue to build upon one another.

• You're more upbeat. One to the drawbacks of remaining closed-minded is that it sometimes contributes to an increase in negativity. Being open will help you develop a more positive outlook on life and the future.

• Expand your knowledge. It's difficult to keep learning when the same old ideas surround you. Pushing your limits and interacting with people who have different viewpoints and experiences will help you keep your mind fresh.

## Factors Affecting Open-Mindedness

A variety of factors may influence a person's openness or closedness to new ideas. While some of the factors that determine how open-minded you are inborn, others can be cultivated to aid in the development of a more open attitude.

## Individuality

According to the five-factor model, one of the five large dimensions that make up human personality is openness to experience. Many of the same characteristics as open-mindedness, such as being able to explore new experiences and concepts and engaging in self-examination, are shared by this personality trait.

## Professionalism

People want experts to be more dogmatic about their field of expertise, according to research. People are less likely to be open-minded when they believe they are more experienced or professional in a particular field than others.

According to researchers, giving participants false positive or false negative feedback about their success on a task affected how closed-minded they were about considering an alternative political viewpoint.

## 1 How Difficult Is It to Become a Professional at Something?

### Comfortable in the Face of Uncertainty

When it comes to coping with confusion, people have different levels of comfort. People get uneasy and even anxious when there is too much uncertainty. Dogmatism is an attempt to keep things straightforward and understandable at times. People may reduce uncertainty and risk — or at least their perception of risk — by dismissing new ideas that could threaten the status quo. Older research backs up this theory, claiming that closed-minded people are less tolerant of cognitive contradictions. 2

### How to Develop a More Open-Minded Attitude

It is possible to learn to be more open-minded, but it can be difficult. Our minds are wired to perceive ideas as wholes in several respects. The psychologist Jean Piaget coined the term "schema" to describe how we create a concept or a category of information. In a conceptual mechanism known as assimilation, we sort new knowledge into one of our current schemas as we come across it.

However, sometimes what we've discovered doesn't quite align with what we already know. In this case, we must change our view of the environment through the accommodation process. To cope with this new knowledge, we must essentially change how we think.

After all, you're only filing new details into your current filing system, so assimilation is usually a simple operation. It's more difficult to find anywhere to stay. You're not just adding something to an existing file; you're starting from scratch.

New knowledge can necessitate rethinking previously held beliefs. It necessitates reassessing your memories and past interactions in light of what you've discovered.

To do so, you must be able to put aside your preconceptions, examine the facts carefully, and confess that you were mistaken. The process can be challenging, perplexing, and even painful or life-altering.

You can train the brain to be more open-minded with a lot of mental effort.

**Confirmation Bias Must Be Overcome**

One of the most significant contributors to closed-mindedness is a cognitive phenomenon known as confirmation bias. Overcoming this tendency, on the other hand, can be difficult. The confirmation bias occurs when we pay more attention to things that support our current convictions while dismissing information that contradicts them.

One of the most effective ways to overcome confirmation bias is to be mindful of it. Take a moment to consider how your bias could influence how you interpret information as you come across it. Take a moment to consider any reasons that could question your beliefs if it appears that you are readily supporting something because it supports your current arguments. It's also beneficial to learn how to analyze sources of knowledge and how to be an educated reader of science news reports.

## How Do Cognitive Biases Affect Your Thinking and Behavior?

### Make Inquiries

The majority of people want to believe in their own intellectual superiority. In many ways, being able to trust and believe in your own decisions is crucial. However, it's important to note that what appears to be a firm commitment to those values can simply be a kind of closed-minded stubbornness.

**Being open-minded includes the ability to challenge not only others but also oneself. Ask yourself a few main questions when you come across new information:**

• How much do you know about the subject?

• How reliable is the source?

• Have you considered any other possibilities?

• Do you have any cognitive biases that may be affecting your decisions?

In certain ways, self-questioning will help you strengthen your commitment to your values. It could also provide you with new perspectives that you hadn't considered before.

**Give it some time.**

Your first reaction might be to disagree or shut down when you hear something you don't agree with. You enter a mode of thought where you are only trying to prove the other person wrong, even before you even have a chance to consider all of the arguments, rather than listening or considering the other viewpoint.

It's easy to get caught up in your emotional reaction to something. You disagree, you don't agree with what you've read, and you might even want the other person to know how much they're mistaken. The problem with that kind of quick-draw answer is that you're reacting in the heat of the moment, not taking the time to think about any of the issues, and you're probably not arguing very well.

Another option is to set aside some time to consider the claims and weigh the proof. Take a few moments after hearing something to consider the following points before responding:

• Do you have several references for your own arguments?

• Are you able to change your mind when confronted with contradictory evidence?

• Would you stick to your convictions even though the evidence contradicts them?

Open-mindedness necessitates a greater mental effort than dogmatism. It's tough enough to be able to accept other points of view, but it's much more difficult when you have to revise your own views as a result.

**Mental Humility should be practiced.**

Even if you consider yourself an expert on a subject, keep in mind that the brain is much more imperfect and imprecise than most of us would like to admit. Being educated about anything can potentially lead to closed-mindedness, according to studies.

People are less likely to accept new knowledge and consider new ideas when they feel they are an expert on a subject or believe they already know everything there is to know. This not only limits the learning ability, but it may also be an indicator of the Dunning-Kruger effect, a cognitive bias. This bias causes people to exaggerate their own knowledge of a topic, oblivious to their own ignorance.

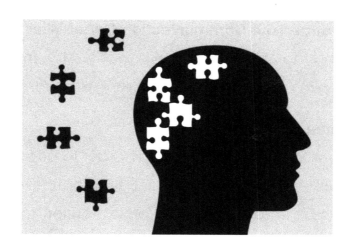

## Communication Skills and Their Importance

Good communication skills are beneficial in all facets of life, from work to personal life, and everything in between. All transactions in business are the product of contact. To allow others and yourself to understand information more accurately and quickly, good communication skills are required.

Bad communication skills, on the other hand, contribute to a lot of confusion and anger. Communication topped the list of the most sought-after soft skills by employers in a 2016 LinkedIn survey conducted in the United States.

## How to Enhance Your Communication Capabilities

When trying to strengthen the ability to interact effectively with others, keep the following in mind:

### 1. Paying attention

It is important to be a good listener in order to become a good communicator. It's important to practice active listening, which entails paying careful attention to what others are saying and clarifying any ambiguities by rephrasing their questions for better comprehension.

### 2. Succinctness

Use as few words as possible to transmit the message. Don't waste time with filler words; instead, get right to the point. The audience will tune out or be unaware about what you're talking about if you ramble. Excessive speaking should be avoided, as should the use of terms that may be confusing to the audience.

### 3. Use of body language

When interacting with others, it is essential to use good body language, maintain eye contact, make hand gestures, and listen to the sound of your voice. A relaxed body posture combined with a welcoming tone can help you appear approachable to others.

In communication, it's important to make eye contact with the other person to show that you're paying attention to what they're saying. However, avoid staring at the individual, as this can make him or her uncomfortable.

## 4. Self-assurance

Be self-assured in what you say and in your relationships with others. Keeping eye contact, maintaining a relaxed body posture, and speaking with precision will all help you feel more confident. Make sure your comments don't sound like questions, and don't try to come across as offensive or demeaning.

## 5. Inquisitiveness

When you don't agree with what someone else says, whether it's a boss, a coworker, or a neighbour, it's important to sympathise with their point of view rather than simply trying to get your point across. Respect other people's opinions and never belittle those who disagree with you.

## 6. be respectful

Respecting and considering what others have to say is an important part of communication. Paying attention to what they have to say, using their name, and not getting disturbed are all examples of being polite. Respecting others makes the other person feel valued, which leads to a more open and fruitful interaction.

## 7. Choosing the right medium

There are many types of communication to choose from; it's crucial to choose the correct one. For example, speaking with someone in person about serious issues (layoffs, pay increases, etc.) is preferable to sending an email.

## Communication Skills for a Successful Career

In order to succeed in your career, you must be able to communicate effectively. You must know what you want and how you want to achieve it. Being a good communicator will help you advance in your career.

Good communication skills will help you get an interview and get through the selection process. Being able to communicate effectively gives you a huge advantage! Discussing issues, requesting information, interacting with others, and having good human relations skills are all part of having good communication skills. They assist in being well understood as well as understanding the needs of those around you.

**In the workplace, there is an insufficient communication.**

Communication is the key to a successful workplace. While the consequences of inadequate communication with others may not be evident immediately, they have a long-term debilitating impact on the workplace. Here are several indicators of a lack of communication:

• Lack of specific contact • Using the wrong mediums to communicate critical messages • Passive-aggressive communication • Lack of follow-through and consideration • Blaming and threatening others

**You Must Learn Communication Skills**

It is not difficult to boost your communication skills and become a conversationalist, in my opinion. However, the only thing that can stop you from progressing is a lack of recognition. You must remember that you must put in effort to improve your communication skills in order to become a successful communicator.

Now it's time to go through the nine essential communication skills that will help you succeed in your career:

**1. Self-assurance**

Confidently expressed ideas and opinions create a better impact on the people with whom you are interacting. Being self-assured demonstrates your authority on the subject and allows the audience to trust your ability.

Maintaining eye contact, maintaining good body posture, and showing appreciation are all ways to demonstrate faith in conversations. All of these items will help you communicate more with your listeners and leave a lasting impression.

If you want to master the art of communication, you must first develop self-confidence. However, there is a fine line between trust and arrogance that you can never cross. It is normal for people who are overconfident to sound more noisy and offensive during a conversation, consider others' thoughts to be inferior, and prove their point aggressively.

2. Respect when you and your audience respect each other, communication is always effective. You should respect the thoughts and views of others during a discussion and allow them to talk freely about whatever is on their mind.

You are completely incorrect if you believe that you are the only one who should be speaking while talking. Communication, as you might have learned, is a two-way street. You must respect and listen to others' thoughts if you want them to respect and listen to yours. Forcing the ideas on others never works out well, and it almost always leads to the breakdown of the whole communication process.

## 3. Paying Attention

The distinction between hearing and listening is important. Because hearing simply involves receiving sound (in the form of words and sentences), listening entails hearing the words and sentences first and then processing them to comprehend their meaning.

Communication, as I previously said, is all about exchanging and receiving knowledge. To understand what others are thinking, you must be an involved listener. You would be unable to comprehend the message if you are just hearing and not listening. As a result, if you talk with others and they notice that you aren't paying attention to what they're doing, the conversation will end quickly.

To become an active listener, you must concentrate on what others are saying and ask questions to comprehend what they are saying fully.

Emotional Intelligence (EQ) is a fourth factor to consider.

Emotional intelligence is the next critical communication ability that you will still need at work. It is the ability to monitor and use one's emotions in order to create a more compelling message.

This ability not only allows you to communicate effectively, but it also allows you to form friendly relationships and express your emotions to others. Sharing your feelings with others can also aid in stress relief and happiness.

Another feature of emotional intelligence is the ability to recognize other people's emotions. When speaking with your employee or colleague, they should feel assured that you can understand and communicate with their emotional state.

Before you dismiss this ability, let me state unequivocally that understanding other people's emotions is difficult. As a result, mastering this ability necessitates both time and patience.

## 5. Volume and Tone

Your voice's sound and volume are critical in creating the right environment for a productive conversation. The sound of your message will have a significant effect on the impression it has on the viewer. To communicate better with your audience, a calm and clear tone of voice is preferred.

The tone, however, can vary depending on the situation. When speaking with a client, you should be cool, while delegating vital tasks to a team member should be firm and authoritative.

Aside from tone, the volume or loudness of your voice is also essential. People would have trouble understanding what you're saying if your voice is too low. On the other hand, a loud speech comes across as rude and appears to irritate the audience.

To make people more comfortable engaging with you, you must balance both the tone and volume of your voice.

### 6. Have open feedback

Feedback, to be honest, can be frightening at times. However, it is a necessary component of successful communication. Critical feedback is often helpful for good communicators because it helps them understand the importance of their message or knowledge.

The response you get from the people with whom you interact is known as feedback. It enables you to determine how well your target audience is receiving your messages. Furthermore, positive feedback identifies ways in which you can develop your communication skills.

During a conversation, you can invite your listeners to share their opinions on the details you're sharing as well as the manner in which you're expressing your thoughts and ideas. This will allow you to get valuable input from the audience and will make it easier for you to identify your communication strengths and weaknesses.

### 7. Willing to Change

It's simple: you can't speak to everybody in the same way. It's important that you choose different communication types based on your target audience. You should determine which communication style is best for a person or a group before engaging with them.

You won't be able to communicate easily with different people if you stick to a single communication style. Aside from the look, you must also be able to communicate in the appropriate manner. When you only need to share a small amount of information, instant messaging and emails are ideal. On the other hand, these modes are ineffective when the knowledge you want to convey is complicated and lengthy. In that case, face-to-face meetings, phone calls, or video conferencing are the best options.

Before you communicate, you can do some research to determine the best communication style and platforms for exchanging knowledge with various people.

### Nonverbal Communication (No. 8)

The verbal and written means of communication are not the only ways to communicate. Nonverbal communication is also a perfect way to express the message effectively. During conversation, visual signals are useful.

Body language, facial expression, eye contact, and other nonverbal cues can help your audience better understand the details you're presenting. You should concentrate on nonverbal communication because your audience recognizes the visual signals you send them, whether deliberately or unintentionally.

### 9. Willingness to Use the Most Up-to-Date Communication Technologies

When it comes to organizational interactions, adopting technology to communicate with your coworkers is a must. To help team members remain linked, most companies now use top networking tools like chat apps, video conferencing software, and so on.

The popularity of digital communication is increasingly increasing, so it's critical that you stay up to date with all of the latest communication technologies. You should be willing to try new ways of communicating and collaborating with your coworkers.

**Effective Communication Obstacles**

Strong communication skills can almost certainly lead to positive outcomes and help you excel in your professional life. However, simply having the right skills isn't enough to ensure that each of your communication sessions runs smoothly.

There are often some kinds of obstacles that obstruct communication's effectiveness. You must be aware of certain communication barriers so that you can recognize them and do whatever possible to remove them.

As a professional, the following are the most popular communication obstacles you will encounter:

## • Cultural and linguistic disparities

This is a popular stumbling block in organizations where people from various backgrounds and cultures collaborate. There are also likely to be language differences among individuals, which will exacerbate the communication gap.

The only way to resolve this obstacle is to value other people's cultures and strive to find common ground to communicate.

## • Making judgments about others

When you expect positive outcomes from a conversation, being judgmental is never a good idea. When you judge others while talking, you're more concerned with judging them and pointing out their flaws than with trying to understand what they're saying.

When discussing something important with others, you must put your personal differences aside and do your best to agree. Judging someone would only stymie the contact and result in a waste of time and resources.

## • Affectionate Lack of Enthusiasm

If you don't believe in the information you're sharing, communication will never be meaningful. When communicating with others, displaying a lack of enthusiasm may have a detrimental effect on them. People can become disengaged if you deliver your messages in a monotone tone with no difference in facial expressions.

By taking an interest in the details you want to exchange, you will break down this contact barrier. You should also be more confident and ensure that your voice tone is not monotonous.

### • Physical Obstacles

The physical environment has a major influence on contact effectiveness. The transmission of information may be hampered by a noisy atmosphere, poor hearing, speech impairments, and other factors.

Although most physical obstacles, such as background noise, can be easily overcome, other problems, such as speech impairments, necessitate extra care.

## Conclusion

Mental models are mental representations of the outside world that humans use all the time when interacting with the environment and its systems. These mental models are part of an underlying framework of related concepts that change over time as individuals gain experience with a system or domain. Video games provide an environment that encourages the creation of complex mental models.

CPSIA information can be obtained
at www.ICGtesting.com
Printed in the USA
BVHW091145030621
608729BV00005B/1654

9 781802 710953